PEERS HELPING PEERS

Program For The Preadolescent

STUDENT WORKBOOK

Judith A. Tindall, Ph.D.
Psychologist, Consultant
Rohen & Associates
Psychological Center
St. Charles, Missouri

Shirley Salmon-White, Ph.D.
Psychologist, Consultant,
School Administrator
Ferguson-Florissant School District
Florissant, Missouri

Routledge
Taylor & Francis Group
New York London

PEERS HELPING PEERS
Program for the Preadolescent
Student Workbook

Content modifications made in second printing

This edition published 2012 by Routledge
Taylor and Francis Group
27 Church Road
Hove
East Sussex BN3 2FA

Taylor and Francis Group
711 Third Avenue
New York, NY 10017

Technical Development: Teresa Araque
Virginia Cooper
Tanya Dalton
Delores Kellogg
Marguerite Mader
Sheila Sheward

LCN: 90-80478

ISBN: 1-55959-010-6

DEDICATION

To our families who have given us the time to share our experiences and knowledge with you. Thank you to our children, Jarrett, Lamont, Amie, Scott, Shannon; and our husbands, Arburn and Dan.

LETTER TO PEER HELPER

Dear Future Peer Helper:

We are pleased that you have decided to learn Peer Helping skills. The skills you will be learning will help you get along better with your friends and family. They also will help you be a more effective peer helper.

First, getting acquainted with other students in your group is important. If you know each other, learning the skills will be more fun. The important step is understanding how to help. All of us have mistaken ideas concerning helping. Hopefully, this section will clear these mistaken ideas.

Listening with your body shows caring and tells other persons that you are with them, you are tuned into them, and you care about them. Your eyes, body posture, and tone of voice all communicate a message.

Listening completely involves accurately hearing the other person's meaning or feelings. To be able to hear another person's feelings you must learn about your own feelings. This is called empathy.

Sending "I" messages is a key skill that will help you express your own feelings and the impact of another person's behavior on you. This is the skill of being assertive. At times, people will need to be confronted and the "I" message will facilitate that.

Helpful questioning is another key basic skill that will facilitate discussion and learning about another person.

At times you will find yourself in conflicts with your friends and family. Conflict resolution skills are important to use as you reduce the conflict between you and another person. The skill is also helpful as you try to help others reduce conflict.

Decision making and goal setting can be good for you to learn and help others.

Next, as you begin to put your skills into action, you must be concerned about several issues such as confidentiality, supervision, practice, school rules, and peer helping guidelines.

To help you keep track of all you have learned, please write your thoughts and feelings in your workbook as you progress in your training. These thoughts and feelings can be a reaction to the activities, how this has affected you, your family, and friends.

Once you have learned key helping skills, you are ready to apply the skills through tutoring, being a special friend, a helper, a playground friend, mediator, conflicts resolver, or a helper in other ways. As you learn how to apply your skills, you are "truly" ready to help others. We want to wish you luck as you start on your journey to becoming a peer helper.

Dr. Judith A. Tindall

Dr. Shirley Salmon-White

CONTENTS

PART I

LEARNING ACTIVITIES

610

You are about to start a program that will help you get along better with yourself, your family, and classmates. You will learn about yourself and how to help others. We believe that the skills you learn will help you in your role as a peer helper and later in life as a worker, parent, and friend. We believe that the first person with whom someone talks to about a concern is a friend, so for peers to talk with peers is natural.

These activities you are starting to experience are different than other activities you do at school in that you will be asked to be involved completely and you will be asked to share about yourself and to practice certain skills.

These activities will help you understand how you can help others, how you can let someone else know you are really listening, and how you can help others resolve disagreements and conflicts. These skills can be used one-on-one with a friend or with a special friend your supervisor has asked you to help. These skills also can be used on the playground, lunchroom, and other areas.

Peer helper training is more than the kind of learning where you sit and listen to a teacher. When each new skill is presented, you will be asked to practice the skill and also do homework. Your leader will demonstrate many of the skills to you before you are asked to do them. You also will receive feedback on the skills from your leader or teacher.

One of the experiences that help you grow is writing daily about your learning and how this applies to your daily life. Please use the space provided in your workbook to write your thoughts and feelings.

To learn the skills you must be actively involved in the activity. We encourage you to become serious about the training. How much you learn depends on you. We want you to look ahead and imagine an exciting fun time in learning human relationship skills. You will find that these skills will help you in many ways for the rest of your life.

Throughout your training you will have an opportunity to hear others share ideas, beliefs, and basic information. You will be able to observe skills as they are demonstrated and practiced. Yes, you will become involved in a very active-interactive means with your leader and your peer helpers who are in training. The basic concepts of tell, show, and involve apply to good learning and helping.

TELL ME

and maybe I'll remember.

SHOW ME

and maybe I'll understand.

INVOLVE ME

and I'll learn, I'll change.

MODULE 1
GETTING ACQUAINTED

GETTING ACQUAINTED

The following activities will help you learn about yourself and others in your peer helping group. The activities help you and other peer helpers know things about each other that only our closest friends and family know. As a result, you will be better able to learn skills in other modules in this book.

Name ______________________________

Date ____________ Hour ____________

Activity 1.1
WARM UP TO GETTING ACQUAINTED

GOAL:

To get to know other peer helpers.

DIRECTIONS:

1. Name the color that most describes you.

   Example: I am the color blue.

   I am the color ______________________________

2. Tell why this color is you.

   Example: I am the color blue, like a mountain lake because my outer self is warm but deep in me is coldness.

   I am the color ____________________ because ____________________

   ____

3. Tell what form you created with your color.

   Example: I am a wrinkled, blue ball.

   ____

   ____

   ____

   ____

   ____

   ____

   ____

   ____

   ____

   ____

Activity 1.2
GETTING ACQUAINTED

GOAL:

To help you develop a personal relationship with other peer helpers.

DIRECTIONS FOR "NAME TAG" ACTIVITY:

1. Cut your name tag into a shape that you like.

2. Draw a symbol or picture on your name tag that tells something special about you.

   Example: Name tag cut in form of football and then name added plus lines to make the name tag resemble a football.

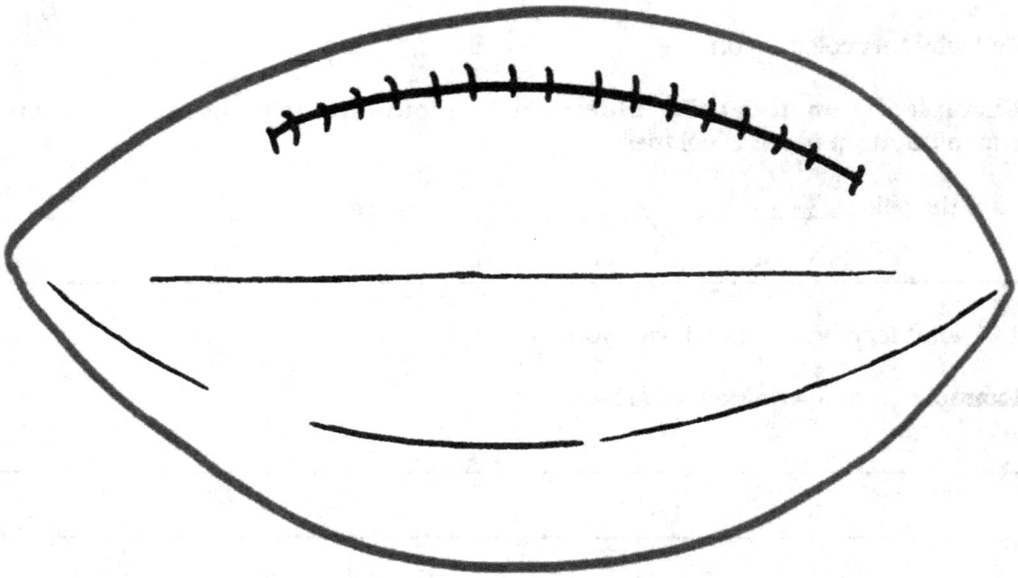

3. Select a partner and see if your partner can guess the meaning of your symbol in the picture.

4. Introduce your partner to the group saying,

   a. your partner's name,

   b. explaining the picture or symbol, and

   c. anything else you learned about your partner as a person.

DIRECTIONS FOR "DRAWING ABOUT YOU" ACTIVITY:

1. Divide a sheet of paper into four parts.
2. Draw something that is very important to you in each part.

   Example:

   Part 1—Family

   Part 2—Computer

   Part 3—Person Working in woods

   Part 4—Radio

3. Find a partner and share your drawing with the partner and what it means.

   Examples:

   I have a brother and a mom and I love to play on computers. I also like to play ball and ride my bike. My favorite way to relax is listening to rock music.

4. Listen carefully to your partner and then share your partner's drawing with the group.

DIRECTIONS FOR "NAME GAME" ACTIVITY:

1. Listen to your leader give directions for you to participate in this activity as a volunteer or as a listener.

2. Say your name and tell something about yourself.

   Example: I am Shirley and I love listening to music.

3. When you finish, throw the imaginary ball to someone else.

4. Listen to each person so you know his or her name.

DIRECTIONS FOR "I AM A PERSON WHO WANTS TO BE A PERSON WHO. . ." ACTIVITY:

1. Write some goals you have for changing yourself during the next few months.

2. Use construction paper to make a kite.

3. Draw or cut out pictures or symbols that describe yourself as you are now. Place these on one side of the kite.

4. On the other side of kite, write, draw, or cut out pictures or symbols that show what your goals are or what you want you to be sometime in the future.

5. Show your kite to your partner and have your partner show his or her kite to you.

6. Introduce each other's kite to the rest of the group.

DIRECTIONS FOR "I AM. . . AND THAT'S . . ." ACTIVITY:

1. Help your group form into a circle.

2. Proceed my giving information about yourself as requested by your leader.

Name ______________________________

Date ____________ Hour ____________

Activity 1.3
BRAG BAG

GOAL:

To build positive self-esteem.

DIRECTIONS:

1. Follow instructions given by your leader as your play the "Brag Bag" game.
2. Write how you felt as you shared good things about yourself.
3. After playing "Brag Bag" with the group, complete the sentences in your own "bag" below.

BRAG BAG

Name ______________________________

I'm really good at ______________________________

____

I'm terrific when I ______________________________

____

I like my self because ______________________________

____

I do a good job at ______________________________

____

I'm a good friend because ______________________________

____

I'm getting better at ______________________________

____

Activity 1.4
CREATING A GREAT GROUP

GOAL:

To set group rules for a great group.

DIRECTIONS:

1. Learn the six "Peer Helping Group Rules"

   a. One person talks at a time.

   b. We listen carefully to the person talking.

   c. We help each other talk openly about our feelings.

   d. We all set weekly goals.

   e. We compliment each other when we show progress.

   f. We keep all group talk to ourselves.

2. Are there any other rules that will help make the group a success? Write them here.

   ____

   ____

   ____

   ____

   ____

3. Sign your name if you will follow these rules when your training starts.

   ____

Name ____________________

Date __________ Hour __________

Activity 1.5
PEAK EXPERIENCE IN AND/OR OUTSIDE OF SCHOOL

GOAL:

To share peak experiences with the group.

INFORMATION:

A peak experience is something you did that made you feel great, made you feel good about yourself and might be one of the happiest experiences of your life.

DIRECTIONS:

1. Discuss with leader's direction about peak experiences.

2. Move into groups of five or six persons and share a peak experience you have had. Remember the "Peer Helper Group Rules." As the peak experiences are shared, have one member to record what is said.

   Example: A peak experience for me was dancing.

3. Have the recorder share some of the peak experiences with the total group.

HOMEWORK:

1. For the next week, write your peak experience for each day.

Day 1 ______________________________

____

Day 2 ______________________________

____

Day 3 ______________________________

____

Day 4 ______________________________

____

Day 5 ______________________________

____

Day 6 ______________________________

____

Day 7 ______________________________

____

2. Summarize what makes a peak experience for you?

Example: A peak experience for me usually involves an experience with my friends.

____

____

____

____

____

____

____

____

____

Name ______________________________

Date ____________ Hour ____________

Activity 1.6
WE ALL HAVE HAD SUCCESS

GOAL:

To be able to show our successes to others.

DIRECTIONS:

1. Discuss as a group Homework, Item 2, from Activity 1.5.
2. Discuss as a group the meanings and examples of success.
3. When asked by your leader to do so, please complete the following:

   a. Record a success you have had in school this last week.

   ____

   ____

   ____

   b. Record a success you would like to have in the next week in school.

   ____

   ____

   ____

HOMEWORK:

1. Keep a record of your successes during this next week. Use the space provided below the example. You will need to think about what the "payoff" of the success is to you as well.

Example:

WEEKLY SUCCESS RECORD

Date	My Success	Payoff
1.		
2.		
3.		
4.		
5.		
6.		
7.		

A success I would like to have is ______________________________

____

I can use others' help by ______________________________

____

2. At the end of the week, review your seven successes and note how much progress you are making both as a peer helper and as a person.

3. Write how you might use the help of others for your successes.

4. Be prepared to submit your homework to your leader during the next meeting.

Name ______________________________

Date ______________ Hour ______________

Activity 1.7
WHAT WORRIES ME THE MOST

GOAL:

To build group trust.

DIRECTIONS:

1. Close your eyes and think about something that worries or upsets you. Make sure this is something that you feel comfortable sharing with the group.

2. Record your worry here:

   Example: I worry about making friends.

   I worry most about ____

   ____

   ____

3. Think about something you can do to make your worry go away.

   Example: My worry: I worry about making good grades in school.

   What I can do: I will talk with my teacher or counselor about learning better study habits.

   My worry ____

   ____

   What I can do: ____

   ____

4. Share under your leader's directions some worries of others and how those people could obtain help.

Activity 1.8
SELF-COMMERCIAL

GOAL:

To build self-esteem.

DIRECTIONS:

1. Think about all the neat things about you.

2. Make a list of the neat things about you.

 ____

 ____

 ____

3. Begin to gather pictures from magazines, newspapers, and other material that you can use to make a commercial about your strong points.

 ____

4. Think about a design, a shape, for your background and how you might paste your pictures to fill up the shape. You may write or draw in your commercial.

5. Sketch an initial idea of your design and what might be located on it.

 Example:

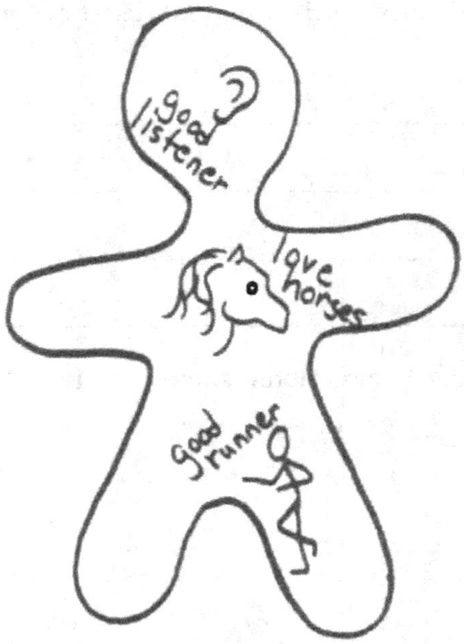

6. Your leader will tell you how to proceed.

Name ______________________

Date ____________ Hour ________

Activity 1.9
BODY TRACING

GOAL:

To build self-esteem.

DIRECTIONS:

1. Move into small groups of three persons.

2. Tape paper on the wall, have one person hold a light, have one person standing facing the paper, between the paper and light, and have the third person trace the silhouette.

   An example may look like this:

3. Cut out your partner. Use paint, crayon, or marker and complete your picture.

   On the back of this sheet sketch your silhouette and try out your coloring before you do it on the large silhouette.

4. If asked to do so by your leader, think about something nice about each member in your group. Be ready to write that nice comment on the body tracing.

SKETCH OF MY SILHOUETTE

Use this space to sketch your silhouette and to try out your coloring proposal before you color the silhouette made in Directions No. 2.

Name ______________________________

Date ____________ Hour ____________

Activity 1.10
SHARING TOPICS

GOAL:

To learn to share on a personal level.

DIRECTIONS:

1. Think about the following three questions. Answer them honestly and write your answers. Be ready to share with others. Write the best thing that happened to you or that you did:

   Last week. ______________________________

   ____

   Over the weekend ______________________________

   ____

   Yesterday ______________________________

   ____

2. Draw a magic box of any shape or size in which you are going to have those things that would make you happy. Space is provided on the back of this sheet for you to draw your magic box and complete Direction No.3.

3. Write or draw in that box a few of those things that would make you extremely happy.

4. Write here about a time when you made someone happy.

   ____

   ____

5. Suppose that your parents had just told you that you were only going to be in this city for one more year.

   a. What would you do differently? ______________________________

   b. How would you change your life? ______________________________

   c. Share and discuss your responses with other members.

MAGIC BOX AND CONTENTS

DIRECTIONS: Follow directions. No. 2 and 3 from preceding page.

Name ______________________

Date ____________ Hour ____________

Activity 1.11
SELF-INVENTORY OF GETTING ALONG WITH OTHERS

GOAL:

To understand better my present way of getting along with others.

DIRECTIONS:

1. Listen to your leader explain each of the things on the "Self-Inventory of Getting Along with Others". Copy is on the back of this sheet.

2. Rate yourself on each numbered entry.

3. Ask someone with whom you have good relationships to give you feedback on these skills.

HOMEWORK:

1. After completing Directions No. 2 and 3, complete the following:

   a. My strengths for getting along with others are

   ____

   ____

   ____

   b. My weaknesses for getting along with others are

   ____

   ____

   ____

   c. I need to change by

   ____

   ____

   ____

2. Discuss at the next session responses with the group.

SELF-INVENTORY OF GETTING ALONG WITH OTHERS

Questions to Ask Myself	The Extent to Which I Do			
	Always	Often	Sometimes	Never
UNDERSTANDING HELPING:				
1. I understand what I can do to be helpful to another person.	____	____	____	____
2. I can say to others when I am tired and that I can't help them now.	____	____	____	____
3. I can explain to others what is meant by helping.	____	____	____	____
TRUST:				
4. When people tell me something, I can keep it to myself.	____	____	____	____
5. If I have to tell someone else, I tell the person first.	____	____	____	____
6. If I tell someone I will do something, I will do it.	____	____	____	____
CARING:				
7. I DO NOT put others down for things they do or say.	____	____	____	____
8. I try to have time to talk with others when they are troubled.	____	____	____	____
ACCEPTANCE:				
9. I try to show others they are OK just the way they are.	____	____	____	____
10. I try not to criticize others.	____	____	____	____

MODULE 2
HELPING PROCESS SKILLS

HELPING PROCESS SKILLS

Being helped by others and helping others can be one of the most rewarding things people can do. Each of us have an opportunity everyday to help classmates, friends, family, and neighbors. When others try to help us, they can either make us feel good or bad. What is it about some people and the way they help that makes us feel good, and why do some of the ways people try to help make us feel bad? For example, you are struggling with trying to understand your math homework and your older sister says, "Here, you'll never understand that . . . . I'll do it." Is this helping or not? Using the same example, let's say your older brother sits down with you and tries to understand your difficulty, works with you, and patiently helps you understand your math. Is this helping or not?

Effective helping involves a variety of skills that most people can learn with practice. You might be involved in a variety of settings where these skills can be helpful. Certain communication skills are important in any helping role. These skills include caring (listening with your body), empathy, sending "I" messages, helpful questioning, solving conflicts, decision making, and goal setting.

HELPING SKILLS

Helping Process Skills

These skills include knowing how you can help others and how others can help you. Being aware of my helping skills is an important aspect of the process.

Caring Skills—Listening With Your Body

These skills involve non-verbal "tuning" into another person. The helper lets the other person know that he or she is really there to help by looking at the person and not allowing other things to interfere.

Empathy Skills

These skills include really listening to another person completely. The helper hears both the feelings people are communicating and the real meaning of the message.

Sending "I" Messages Skills

These skills will enable you to let others know when and how they are upsetting you. When they do, you will learn to be more assertive in positive ways.

At times learning to send "I" messages in an assertive manner cannot only let people know how they are affecting you but also help them change their behavior.

Helpful Questioning Skills

These helpful skills are used to assist others in understanding and clarifying their messages.

Conflict Resolving Skills

At times, you may need to help others solve conflicts. By utilizing skills you have learned, you can help others prevent and solve conflict situations.

Decision-Making and Goal-Setting Skills

The ability to problem solve is an important part in helping others. At times, you may be called upon to help friends handle problems that are bothering them and you might help figure out the best solution. You will be assisted in establishing realistic goals.

BEING A PEER HELPER

As a result of these key-helping skills, a variety of roles are served as a helper.

You might want to be a good listener to a classmate. You might want to be an effective helper to a friend, and you might want to help others in your family. You might want to help others learn difficult material, and you also might want to help others through leading a discussion group.

Just picture, if you would, an eight year old girl that is very small for her age. She has trouble with some of her work and she doesn't dress like the other students. Some ten year old boys are making fun of her, and she runs away and hides. You look at her and decide to go talk to her. You try to listen to her and really understand how hurt and upset she is at the boys and how badly she feels because she is different. Finally, she is glad you took the time to talk with her and you join her in the lunch room to be a special friend for a while.

These activities that follow, along with your group class experiences, will help you as you take a journey to learn effective helping skills.

Name ______________________________
Date ______________ Hour ______________

Activity 2.1
HOW OTHERS HELP ME

GOALS:

1. To understand better how others help me.

2. To learn different parts of helping.

DIRECTIONS:

1. Identify one or two people with whom you like to talk that help you feel better after talking with them.

   a. ______________________________

   b. ______________________________

2. Describe some ways this helpful person behaves.

3. In the group, sit quietly and close your eyes when asked by your leader, who will help you imagine a time that you were truly helped by someone else.

4. Open your eyes and draw, in the space provided on back of this sheet, a picture of the "helpful person" or identify characteristics of the helpful person. Color the picture or relate color to each characteristic to give it more expression. Respond to the questions about your helper.

5. Turn to the page entitled "Imagery Experience" and complete the sheet.

6. Complete the "Helper List" sheet included in this exercise.

7. Share with the group the characteristics of helpers found on "Helper List."

8. Share with the group what have you learned about effective helping.

HOMEWORK:

1. Write a short paragraph and describe a time when someone helped you with a problem.

   An example might be when you were angry at someone because they let you down. You were hurt because you were left out. Describe what the other person did that was helpful. What did that person look like while they were helping you and what were your thoughts and feelings about the helper?

2. Be prepared to submit your homework to your leader at the next meeting.

MY PICTURE
OF
A HELPFUL PERSON

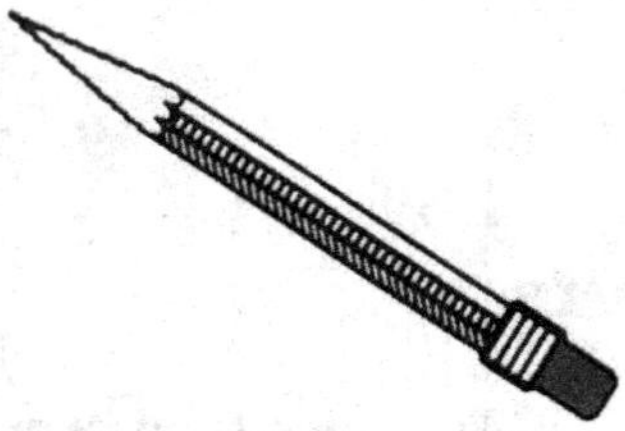

Name ______________________________
Date ______________ Hour ______________

IMAGERY EXPERIENCE
A PICTURE OF SOMEONE HELPING ME

REACTIONS TO THE IMAGE

1. Describe the experience: ______________________________

2. My energy level during the experience was ______________

3. My concentration was ______________________________

4. The strengths of my helper were ______________________________

5. I felt ______________________________

HELPER LIST

Think of some "helpful people" and, if possible, identify one who has been helpful with or for you. Then complete the following information.

	Names of People	Body Talk	What They Said to Help	What They Did to Help
1.	____________	____________	____________	____________
2.	____________	____________	____________	____________
3.	____________	____________	____________	____________
4.	____________	____________	____________	____________
5.	____________	____________	____________	____________

Name ______________________
Date ____________ Hour ____________

Activity 2.2
WHO CARES FOR ME

GOALS:

1. To help you find people to whom you can talk who will be supportive, caring, and understanding in most situations.

2. To know the kinds of feelings you have when you need to seek the assistance of someone else.

DIRECTIONS:

1. Recall some strong feelings you have had recently.

   Example: Hurt because I was not invited to a friend's house.

2. Make a list of those feelings and share with your leader.

3. Participate in a discussion about the following questions:

   What was happening when you felt that way?

   How did you know you were feeling that way?

   How did you let other people know how you were feeling?

   Would you react the same way again?

4. Compile a list of people with whom you would choose to share the above feelings. Record your list on the page entitled "My Support Group List" in the column entitled "Present People."

5. Keep this list and add to it as the peer helping training progresses.

HOMEWORK:

Think of additional times you may need support and someone to talk with and expand your list of support people. List some people you would like to have on your list. Place those people in column "Possible Future Support People" in the "My Support Group List."

MY SUPPORT GROUP LIST

List people with whom you would be able now to share your feelings. Place their names in the column marked "Present People." Then think of people with whom you would like to be able to share in the future. Add their names in the last column on the right.

Environment	Present People	Possible Future Support People
School		
Home		
Play		

Name ______________________________

Date ______________ Hour ______________

Activity 2.3
UNDERSTANDING HOW I HELP

GOALS:

1. To become aware of my natural helping skills.
2. To develop a definition of helping.

DIRECTIONS:

1. Think of two to five times you have helped another person in the last week.

   Examples:

   a. Listened to a friend with a problem.

   b. Listened to someone within your family that was angry.

2. On the page entitled "People I Have Helped and My Feelings" identify in column one the two to five people from Direction 1.
3. In column two of the page "People I Have Helped and My Feelings" make a list of specific things you did trying to help the persons listed in column one.

   Examples:

   a. Sat next to them.

   b. Paid attention.

   c. Let the other person talk.

4. In column three and four, write feelings during and after helping.

5. Share with other members in your peer helping group your list of specific things you do to try to help others.

6. Assemble into subgroups of three:

   One person to be the listener
   One person to be the talker
   One person to write down what was said

   Each person is to talk about his or her own definition of helping. Include characteristics and behaviors that you do when you try to help. One person writes a summary of the discussion.

   Exchange roles so each person has the opportunity to play all three roles.

7. Develop within your subgroup a definition of helping.

8. Write your subgroup's definition on the sheet entitled "Definition of Helping."

9. Share your subgroup's definition of helping with your whole training group.

10. Record two or three definitions of helping that you like that were developed by other subgroups.

HOMEWORK:

Look over a list of definitions of helping that each subgroup developed and write on the sheet entitled "Definition of Helping" the one that means the most to you.

Name ______________________________

Date ______________ Hour ______________

PEOPLE I HAVE HELPED AND MY FEELINGS

Name of Person	What I Did	My Feelings During Helping	Feelings After Helping

DEFINITIONS OF HELPING

What Others Say as Helping:

A helpful person is someone that communicates to people being helped that they truly care, accept other people just as they are, and show they can be trusted.

1. Our group's definition is ____

____

____

____

2. Record two or three definitions of helping that you like that were developed by other groups.

____

____

____

____

HOMEWORK:

My own definition of helping is ______________________________

____

____

____

Name ______________________

Date ____________ Hour ____________

Activity 2.4
SELF-INVENTORY OF HELPING SKILLS

GOAL:

To understand better my present helping skills.

DIRECTIONS:

1. Listen to your leader explain each of the things on the "Self-Inventory of Helping Skills."
2. Rate yourself on each numbered entry.
3. Ask someone whom you have helped to give you feedback on these skills.

HOMEWORK:

1. Look at each area in which you already do well and list two or more of your strengths. ______________________

   ____
2. Look at each area in which you need to improve and list two or more of your weaknesses. ______________________

   ____
3. List two or more improvement goals for training in helping skills. ____________

   ____
4. List some ways (make a plan) for achieving the goals in Item 3. ____________

   ____

SELF-INVENTORY OF HELPING SKILLS

QUESTIONS TO ASK MYSELF	The Extent to Which I Do			
	Always	Often	Sometimes	Never
Caring Skills—Listening With My Body:				
1. My body shows I am listening.				
2. I look at the person talking.				
3. I am not trying to do something else when I talk with them.				
4. I lean toward another person when I am listening.				
5. My body is relaxed.				
6. I concentrate on what others are saying.				
Empathy Skills:				
7. I understand the words people say.				
8. I understand the feelings others have.				
9. I do not guess the inner feelings or thoughts of others.				
10. I can repeat in my own words what others are saying.				
11. I understand what others are saying.				
Helpful Questioning Skills:				
12. When I ask questions, people continue talking for a long time.				
13. When I ask questions, people explain more of what they mean				
Sending "I" Message Skills:				
14. I can say "no" if I don't want to do something.				
15. I can say how I feel about another's behavior.				
16. I can say how another's behavior effects me.				
17. I can say to another person what I want to do.				
18. I can say to another person what I need.				
Resolving Conflict Skills:				
19. I can let someone know if what they are saying or doing is different.				

Name ______________________________

Date ____________ Hour ____________

SELF-INVENTORY OF HELPING SKILLS

QUESTIONS TO ASK MYSELF	The Extent to Which I Do: Always	Often	Sometimes	Never
20. I can let others know how they behave.				
21. I can imagine solving conflicts.				
22. I can use my skills to solve conflicts.				
Problem-Solving and Goal-Setting Skills:				
23. I can help others understand the problem.				
24. I can help people understand what they are trying to solve.				
25. I can help others explore all different parts of the problem.				
26. I can help others think of different solutions to the problem.				
27. I can help the person select the best solution.				
My Helping Roles:				
28. I know how to perform my helping roles.				
29. I can be a good tutor.				
30. I can be a good listener.				
31. I can be a good group leader.				
32. I can be a good listener in my family.				
33. I can be a good listener to others.				
34. I follow roles of helping.				

Activity 2.5
MY CONTRACT FOR LEARNING HELPING SKILLS

GOALS:

1. To develop a contract for learning helping skills.
2. To understand my own limitations.

DIRECTIONS:

1. Discuss with your group and leader the importance of contracts in peer helping work.
2. Review the "Peer Helping Contract" and recognize the behaviors that will be expected of you as a member of the peer helping training group.
3. Review your notes in Activity 2.4 which will be valuable for this activity.
4. Make a list of behaviors you are going to practice.
5. Work with your leader and your other peer helpers as you identify items to place in a contract for you to learn to overcome your limitations.
6. Record your plan on the sheet entitled "My Learning Contract."
7. Review with your leader those items on your contract and come to an agreement on the items listed.
8. Sign "My Learning Contract" and the "Peer Helping Contract" and have your leader to review and, if the two of you are in agreement, have the leader sign.

Name ____________________

Date ____________ Hour ____________

PEER HELPING CONTRACT

I agree to

1. Attend and be on time to all training meetings.
2. Listen to others in my training group.
3. Listen carefully to my trainer.
4. Practice the skills learned in training.
5. Share important things about myself.
6. Help others set goals.
7. Keep what others have said to myself.
8. Complete homework assignments.
9. Come to training alert and free from drugs and alcohol.
10. Give feedback to others in my group.
11. Other agreements: ______________________________

____

Signature of Peer Helper: ______________________________

Signature of Leader: ______________________________

Date: ____________________

MY LEARNING CONTRACT

My Contract For Training as a Peer Helper

I agree to

1. ____
____
____

2. ____
____
____

3. ____
____
____

4. ____
____
____

5. ____
____
____

My Signature: ______________________________________

Signature of Leader: ________________________________

MODULE 3
CARING SKILLS

Listening With Your Body

CARING SKILLS

Listening With Your Body

As we begin to help others, we need to understand that our body language can communicate that we care and want to help. Some researchers say most of what we communicate is through our own body language. What we say in words is often not as important as what our body says. Some of you can recall times in your life in which it felt good just to get a hug. The other person didn't have to say they cared. You also can remember a time when you knew you were in trouble based on the look of the face of a parent or teacher. You may be able to recall a time when you didn't trust a friend because what they said was different than what they looked like.

You may be able to know how a person is feeling by looking at him or her. As we truly try to care for (listen, attend) another person, we need to "tune" into them by

LOOKING AT THE PERSON,

RELAXING OUR BODIES,

LOOKING CONFIDENT,

HAVING OUR BODIES LOOK OPEN, and

SHOWING CARE AND CONCERN ON OUR FACES.

The following activities will help you focus on attending skills and also help you pick up on the body language in others.

Name ______________________________

Date ______________ Hour ______________

Activity 3.1
BODY LANGUAGE WARM-UP

GOAL:

To practice communicating with body language.

DIRECTIONS:

1. Listen to the leader explain different types of communication.
2. Follow the leader's directions concerning body language activity.
3. Discuss the different types of communication that were used during the activity.
4. Record one learning you had about a feeling shown through a nonverbal behavior.

Activity 3.2
WHAT OTHERS COMMUNICATE THROUGH BODY LANGUAGE

GOALS:

1. To learn what others are saying by their body language.

2. To tune in on what others communicate by body language.

DIRECTIONS:

1. Brainstorm (think quickly) feeling words and explain how these feelings are shown by our bodies.

2. Look through magazines and other items you and your leader have brought to class.

3. Cut out pictures and identify what the person is saying and feeling by the picture.

   Example: This person looks happy and maybe just did something great.

4. Look for pictures that represent:

   Happy

Glad

Name ______________________________

Date ______________ Hour ______________

Frustrated

Angry

Fearful

5. Show the pictures to the group.

6. Pantomime feelings to the group and have group members guess what feeling is being pantomimed.

HOMEWORK:

1. Observe the body language of someone you care about and with whom you have contact often and keep a list of feelings you observe. Try to notice what is going on. Ask the person if you guessed the feelings correctly.

2. Record your observations.

What was person doing at the time you were watching?	What body movement did you see?	What did the body movement mean?	Were you correct?

3. Write what you learned from this activity.

____

____

____

____

____

____

____

____

Name ______________________________

Date _______________ Hour _______________

Activity 3.3
TUNE IN TO OTHERS

GOAL:

To learn to look at the facial characteristics of others and to learn to tune in to others.

DIRECTIONS:

1. Think of times when you felt afraid and list some. Do not show your list to others.

   Example: Storming at night.

2. Think of times when you were happy and list some. Keep your list secret.

   Example: Vacation, received a gift, got a hug.

3. Think of a time you felt proud and list some. Keep your list secret.

   Example:

   a. Just got a good grade.

   b. Just received an award.

4. Divide into groups of threes and have one person close his or her eyes and think about a time he or she felt afraid, happy, and proud. Think about each one for only five seconds.

   The two observers are to guess in what order you imaged each one.

   As the person doing the imaging, you do not have to tell specifically what you were thinking about, but just if they observed the correct feeling.

5. Change so all have a chance to participate.

6. Share with the large training group what you learned as you tuned in to others.

Activity 3.4
COMPARING NONATTENDING TO ATTENDING

GOAL:

To learn the difference between attending and nonattending.

DIRECTIONS:

1. Observe your leader as nonattending is demonstrated to another person.
2. Divide into groups of two and practice not attending to your partners while your partner talks about something important.
3. Change roles.
4. Discuss as a group how "not attended to" feels.
5. Observe as your leader demonstrates good attending skills.
6. Divide into groups of two and practice using attending while the person is talking about something that is important.
7. Change roles.
8. Share as a group how being "attended to" feels and compare with how you felt when not being attended to.

HOMEWORK:

1. In the following space write your personal feelings:

   a. When your partner was not paying attention to you.

   ____

   ____

   b. When your partner was paying attention to you.

   ____

   ____

Name ______________________

Date ____________ Hour ____________

2. During the next day or two notice attending and nonattending behavior in school, home, or other places such as grocery store, restaurant, or playground. Write your observations in the space provided.

a. Attending Behavior ______________________

____

Situation or scene: ______________________

____

____

Descriptions of behavior: ______________________

____

____

Result as you saw it: ______________________

____

____

b. Non-attending Behavior ______________________

____

Situation or scene: ______________________

____

____

Description of behavior: ______________________

____

____

Result as you saw it: ______________________

____

____

Activity 3.5
PRACTICE EFFECTIVE ATTENDING

GOALS:

1. To practice nonverbal listening.

2. To obtain feedback on skills in nonverbal listening.

DIRECTIONS:

1. Observe your leader demonstrating effective attending and identify attending skills demonstrated.

2. Divide into groups of three and then you or one of the others in your group needs to talk about one of the following topics:

   a. how other people show they care,

   b. how I show I accept others just as they are, or

   c. how do I show others I am interested in them.

3. One person within your group of three is to play the helper and try to use good body communication.

4. The third person gives feedback in nonverbal skills using the "Observer Feedback Form."

5. Change roles until all have had a chance to play all three roles.

6. Discuss your experiences with the total group.

Name ______________________

Date ____________ Hour ____________

OBSERVER FEEDBACK FORM

Name of Listener: ______________________________________

Directions: As an observer, check (X) the following as to what the listener does while the other person talks.

	NO	PRETTY MUCH	YES
1. Looked interested	____	____	____
2. Looked relaxed	____	____	____
3. Looked concerned	____	____	____
4. Eyes steady	____	____	____
5. Facial expression calm	____	____	____
6. Other ______________	____	____	____

____

____

Activity 3.6
COMMUNICATION AND LISTENING

GOAL:

To help you understand different types of communication and the importance of listening.

DIRECTIONS:

1. Participate in a role-playing activity that your leader will discuss with you and afterwards discuss what occurred and how you felt.

2. Listen carefully as your leader reads a paragraph to you. Then answer the following questions on the listening test.

LISTENING TEST ANSWER SHEET

a. What is the number of your bus? ______________________

b. When will it pick you up at home? ______________________

c. What time does school begin? ______________________

d. Where is your homeroom? ______________________

e. What time does lunch start? ______________________

f. How long is lunch? ______________________

g. Where do you go after lunch? ______________________

h. What time is recess? ______________________

i. Who is your music teacher? ______________________

j. What time does school end? ______________________

k. How long is recess? ______________________

l. How many answers did you hear accurately? ______________

You might want to take this again at the end of training.

3. List as many things as you can as to what a good listener does.

____

____

____

____

Name ____________________

Date ____________ Hour ____________

4. List as many things as you can that interfere with listening.

____

____

____

____

5. Write one thing you could do to be a better listener and then consider this as a goal for you to achieve.

____

____

____

____

HOMEWORK:

1. Please complete each sentence using as a stem or lead in "I Communicate in Different Ways with Different People"

   a. With my family I . . . . ______________________________

   ____

   ____

   b. With someone I don't know I . . . . ______________________________

   ____

   ____

   c. With my best friend I . . . . ______________________________

   ____

   ____

   d. With my teacher I . . . . ______________________________

   ____

   ____

2. Please complete the following sentences in response to the question "How Do I Feel?"

a. When people don't listen to me I feel . . . . ______________________________

____

____

b. When I have trouble communicating what I really mean, I feel . . . . ______________

____

____

c. When I really think about the person I'm communicating with, I . . . . ____________

____

____

d. I like to listen when . . . . ______________________________

____

____

e. The people I like to talk to best are the ones who . . . . ______________________

____

____

MODULE 4
EMPATHY
SKILLS

EMPATHY SKILLS

Empathy means that we are accurately hearing both the meaning and feeling of others. This module will help you to understand some important facts about not only hearing the words of others but also understanding the meaning and feelings behind those words.

Obviously, if we can think faster than others talk, there is plenty of time to allot ourselves to think of other things, unless we are really trained to listen actively to another person. People often are unskilled in how to grasp meaning and feelings of others as they talk.

This module will help you practice your skills in empathy by learning to accurately recognize some of your feelings and those feelings and thoughts of others.

Name ______________________

Date ____________ Hour ____________

Activity 4.1
THE RUMOR GAME

GOAL:

To learn accurately the meaning of what others are saying.

DIRECTIONS:

1. Consider volunteering to be part of a rumor clinic. Out of your total group, five of you will be needed.
2. Have four of the five volunteers to leave the room and have one to remain in the room.
3. If you are one of those in the room, participate in the rumor clinic game. The leader will tell a story to the one left in the room and that person will repeat it to the next one and so on until everyone has been told the rumor. The last person repeats the rumor to the rest of the students. Do not ask questions.
4. Be an observer if you are not one of the five volunteers.
5. Listen to the accuracy of what the leader told the first student and each student after this.
6. Try to think of ways that the listener might ask questions or clarify the situation.
7. Change roles so that another group of five volunteer and repeat Directions 1 through 6.
8. Discuss as a group
   a. How could the paraphrasing of the listener been improved?
   b. Was it difficult to try to remember and tell the next person?
   c. What happens from the first paraphrase to the last?
   d. How does this happen in our daily life?

HOMEWORK:

1. Try to listen accurately to things that others tell you.

2. Try to paraphrase (place in your words) what they have said and notice their acceptance of your statement.

3. How well are you able to paraphrase? ____

4. Are you able to include in your paraphrase meanings and feelings as you perceive them? __________

   Write illustrations of

   a. What was said ____

   ____

   b. Your paraphrased response ______________________________________

   ____

5. When you do, are your paraphrases generally accepted? _____________________

   Write an illustration of how you know _____________________________________

   ____

   ____

Name ______________________

Date ____________ Hour ____________

Activity 4.2
LEARNING TO PARAPHRASE MEANING

GOAL:

To learn how to communicate through paraphrasing the meaning of a statement.

DIRECTIONS:

1. Discuss with your leader and group members the meaning and value of paraphrasing a statement.

2. Observe the leader demonstrating paraphrasing a statement.

3. Work in large group where one person makes a statement and a person sitting next to him or her responds by paraphrasing the content of the statement.

   Hint: You might want to begin paraphrasing by

   You mean. . . . .

   It sounds like. . . . .

   I hear you saying. . . . .

4. Continue activity until all are able to paraphrase the meaning of one statement.

5. Then work as a group to answer the following:

   Examples:

   a. Person Needing Help: "I am so upset at my friend for talking behind my back to the point I don't want to be friends with her anymore."

Helper Response: (Using paraphrased meaning only) "You mean that you don't want to be friends anymore with your friend because she talks behind your back."

b. Person Needing Help: "I am really having trouble learning my math this year. No matter what I do it doesn't seem to sink in."

Helper Response (paraphrase meaning only) ______________________________

____

____

c. Person Needing Help: "I wish my brother would stay out of all my stuff in my room. He is always getting into my things and throwing them all over the floor and I can't find them. Mom won't do anything about it and says it is my room and my problem . . . "

Helper Response (paraphrase meaning only): ______________________________

____

____

HOMEWORK:

1. Try later today to paraphrase just the meaning of at least one person. Record your experience here.

   a. Person's comments: ______________________________

   ____

   ____

   b. My paraphrase: ______________________________

   ____

   ____

   c. Person's reaction to my comments: ______________________________

   ____

   ____

2. Submit your homework to your leader at the next meeting.

Name ______________________________

Date ______________ Hour ______________

Activity 4.3
LEARNING TO PARAPHRASE FEELINGS

GOAL:

To learn how to hear feelings of another person.

DIRECTIONS:

1. Listen as your leader explains paraphrasing feelings. If you do not understand, ask questions.

2. Observe the leader demonstrating paraphrasing feeling to one statement.

3. Work in a large group where one person makes a statement and the person sitting next to him or her responds by paraphrasing the feeling of what was said. You might want to begin paraphrasing the feeling by saying:

   a. You feel . . . . .

   b. It sounds like you feel . . . . .

   c. I hear you expressing feelings of . . . . .

4. Continue until all are able to paraphrase the feeling of another.

5. Group into small groups of two or three. Study example a and then complete responses for examples b and c.

   Example:

   a. Person Needing Help: "I am so upset at my friend for talking behind my back to the point I don't want to be friends with her anymore."

      Helper Response (paraphrased feeling only): "You are really disappointed with your friend."

   b. Person Needing Help: "I am really having trouble learning my math this year. No matter what I do, it doesn't seem to sink in."

      Helper Response (Use paraphrasing of feeling only): ______________________________

      ____

      ____

      ____

      ____

c. Person Needing Help: "I wish my brother would stay out of all my stuff in my room. He is always getting into my things and throwing them all over the floor and I can't find them. Mom won't do anything about it and says it is my room and my problem. . . . . . "

Helper Response (paraphrase feeling only): ____________________

____

____

____

____

HOMEWORK:

1. Keep an entry of a situation in which you paraphrased feelings within the next day or two:

a. Record a statement someone made where a feeling was shown.

____

____

____

b. Your paraphrase of feeling and meaning.

____

____

____

c. The reaction of the person after your paraphrase. Write how the person looked and what the person said.

____

____

____

2. Be prepared to submit your homework to your leader at the next meeting.

Name ______________________________

Date ______________ Hour ______________

Activity 4.4
THE WORLD IS A STAGE

GOAL:

To develop a broader vocabulary of feeling words.

DIRECTIONS:

1. Watch your trainer write feeling words on the board and help your trainer define each word.

2. Pick one feeling word to role-play to illustrate the feeling. Work individually or with a partner to plan the role-play.

   Example: fear—you might want to think about a time you were afraid of noises in your house late at night. How did you react to the noises?

3. Demonstrate your feeling word to the rest of the group.

4. Have the rest of the group guess the feeling word you are demonstrating.

5. Discuss ways each feeling was demonstrated.

6. Identify essential elements of each feeling.

FEELING BOX

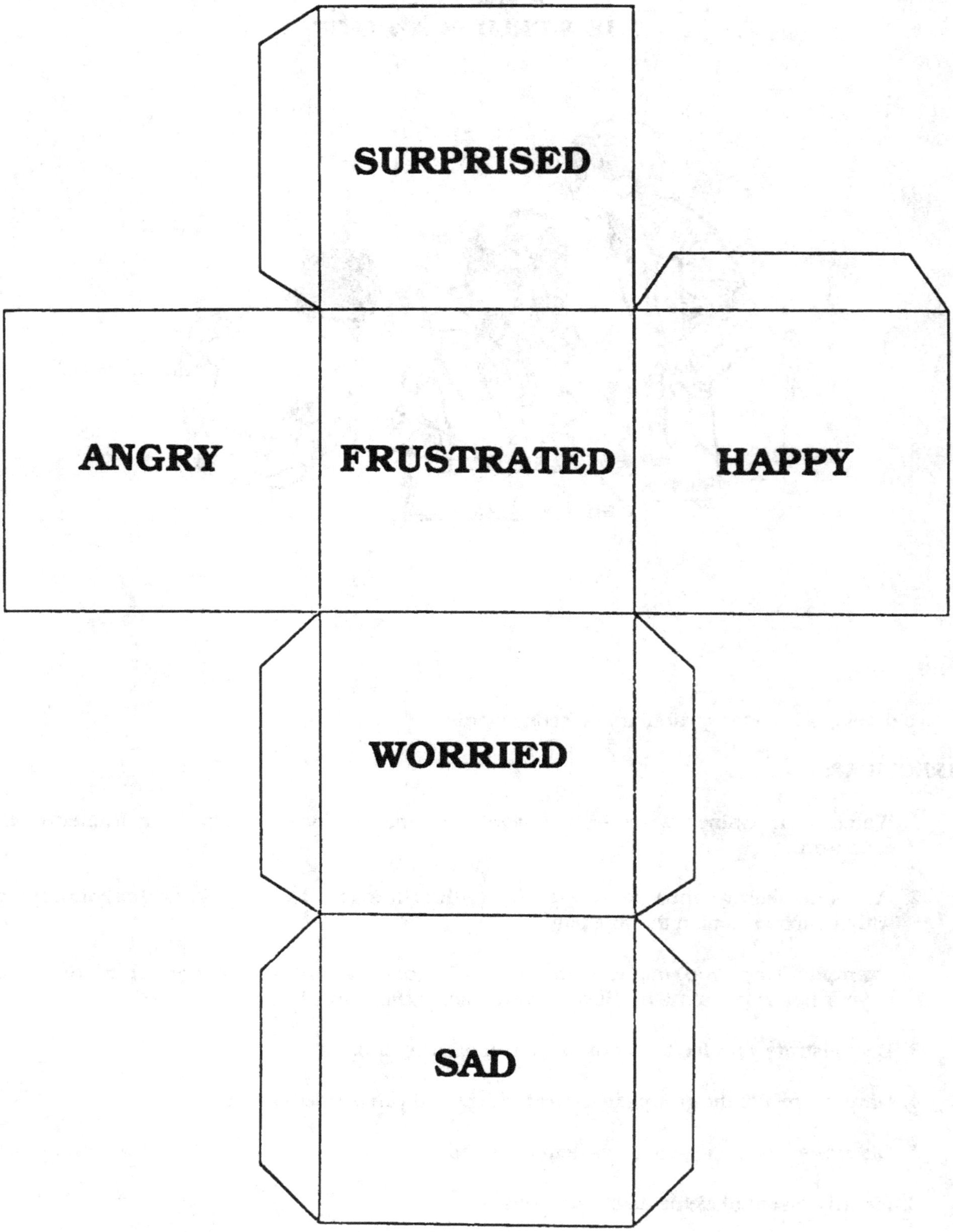

Name ______________________________

Date ______________ Hour ____________

Activity 4.5
ROLLING THE FEELING BOX

GOAL:

To help acquaint you with the connection between feelings and behavior.

DIRECTIONS:

1. Look at the pictures of the different kinds of basic feelings as your leader shows those different feelings.

2. Define each feeling.

   a. Angry ______________________________

   ____

   b. Frustrated ______________________________

   ____

   c. Happy ______________________________

   ____

   d. Suprised ______________________________

   ____

   e. Sad ______________________________

   ____

   f. Worried ______________________________

   ____

3. Try to discuss the feelings in a variety of situations and identify what influences each feeling.

   Examples: For each of the following situations, name the feelings generally associated with each.

   a. Put-downs ______________________________

   b. Stress ______________________________

   c. Compliments ______________________________

d. Sickness ____________________

e. Others (list) ____________________

4. Think of how feelings are decided by yourself or others.

5. Discuss why the identification of your own feelings as they occur is so important.

6. Related to different feelings as you identify them in yourself, write possible things you might do to help yourself and/or prevent you from saying or doing things that might be harmful to others.

   a. Sad—avoid conflict situations

   (other action) ____________________

   ____

   b. Scared—talk with someone

   (other action) ____________________

   ____

   c. Mad— ____________________

   ____

   d. Frustrated— ____________________

   ____

   e. Other feelings (list) ____________________

   ____

7. Discuss why it is difficult to be aware of some feelings.

8. Cut out the feeling box and glue it together.

9. Work in groups of four or five and role the boxes and make the statement of the form below according to the face of the box that is up after you roll the box.

   "I felt ____________________ when ____________________."

10. Discuss the activity in the large group.

HOMEWORK:

Be aware of how you feel this week and report back feelings that you have had and how you behaved. Record three "feeling times."

I felt ____________ when ____________, and I did the following after I recognized my feeling ____________________.

I felt ____________ when ____________, and I did the following after I recognized my feeling ____________________.

I felt ____________ when ____________, and I did the following after I recognized my feeling ____________________.

Name ______________________________

Date ______________ Hour ______________

Activity 4.6
ASSESSING THE FEELING OF HAPPINESS

GOAL:

To help you understand happiness.

DIRECTIONS:

1. Discuss the homework from Activity 4.5.

2. Fill out the assessment activities for feeling happiness.

   a. Complete "Happy Times."

   b. Complete "Year 'Round Happiness."

3. Discuss in the group the assessment activities after you have completed them.

HOMEWORK:

1. Conduct a "Happiness Survey" by asking four people to name three things that make them happy. Record their answers in the blossom.

2. Cut out the blossoms and at the next class meeting add them to the "Tree of Happiness" bulletin board in the classroom.

HAPPY TIMES

I am happy when

1. ____

____

2. ____

____

3. ____

____

4. ____

____

5. ____

____

Put a star (★) before the sentence that tells when you are **most** happy.

Name ______________________________

Date ________________ Hour ________________

YEAR 'ROUND HAPPINESS

Listed below are the four seasons of the year. What is something that happens in each of these seasons that makes you happy?

WINTER

____

____

____

____

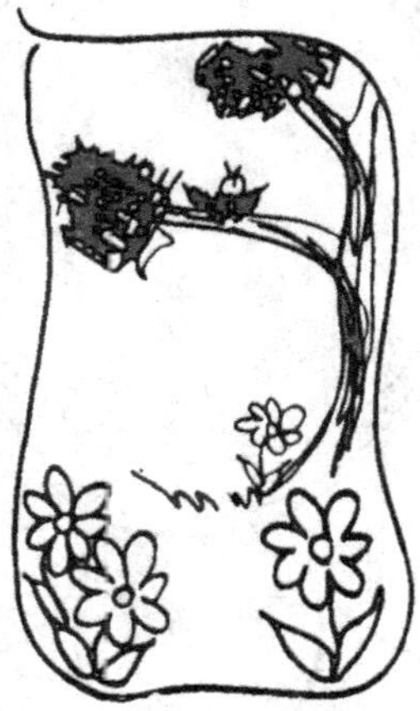

SPRING

____

____

____

____

SUMMER

____

____

____

____

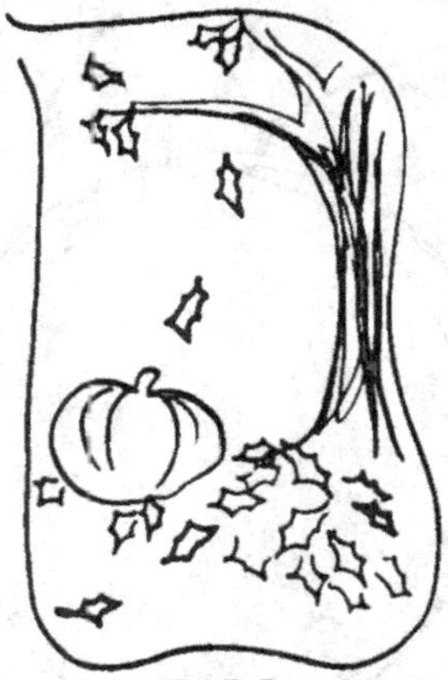

FALL

____

____

____

____

HAPPINESS SURVEY

Name ______________________________

Date ______________ Hour ______________

Activity 4.7
FEELING HAPPY

GOAL:

To help understand the things that make me feel glad and happy.

DIRECTIONS:

1. Add the blossoms from Homework, Activity 4.6 to the "Tree of Happiness."

2. Discuss the "Tree of Happiness" and what you have learned.

3. Discuss the meaning of happiness.

4. Discuss what is different when we feel happy than when we feel sad.

5. Discuss what happens to our bodies when we feel happy.

6. Cite examples of how people react to you when you act happy or glad. Happiness can be contagious.

   Example: If I smile at someone, generally they smile back.

7. Break into goups of three and share the following:

   a. A time someone made me happy.

   b. A time I made someone happy.

8. Fill out "The Happy Me" sheet. Continue in your small group and share your answers.

THE HAPPY ME

It makes me happy to see ____________________

It makes me happy to hear ____________________

It makes me happy to taste ____________________

It makes me happy to smell ____________________

I am happy when I touch ____________________

I am the happiest when ____________________

____

____

____

One of the happiest days I can remember is ____________________

____

____

____

I expect to have a happy time when ____________________

____

____

____

Name ______________________________

Date ______________ Hour ______________

Activity 4.8
PRACTICING BEING HAPPY

GOAL:

To help you practice being happy.

DIRECTIONS:

1. For the next week, look at yourself in a mirror. Practice smiling and looking happy. Walk and hold your body in a happy way. Remember how looking happy feels. Try looking and feeling happy many times throughout the day.

2. Thinking happy thoughts—For the next week before you get up in the morning, lie back and let your body relax. Make a mental list of happy thoughts. Let them go through your mind. Then say to yourself at least three times:

   "I feel happy today."

   "This is going to be a good day."

   "I feel good all over."

   And write your own "Happy Thoughts" on the picture.

3. At the end of seven days, evaluate the week to see if your choice to be happy actually made you feel and be happier. Keep a record in this workbook.

4. State your evaluation below:

   When I practiced looking and acting happy, I felt

1	2	3	4
Sad	The Same	A Little Happier	A Lot Happier

5. Write what you have learned about yourself from this activity: ____________________

____

____

____

____

6. Discuss these activities at the next class meeting.

"HAPPY THOUGHTS"

Name ______________________

Date ____________ Hour ____________

Activity 4.9
STEPS TO HAPPINESS

GOAL:

To help you understand all the things that make you happy.

DIRECTIONS:

1. Discuss "Happy Thoughts" from Activity 4.8.
2. On the sheet of keys, color the ones that are most important to you.
3. Glue them on your "Ladder to Happiness" in order of least important (bottom of ladder) to most important (top of ladder). Continue to climb the ladder by setting your priorities for happiness. The top rung of the ladder should indicate your most important means of happiness. Share your ladder with your group.
4. Cut out the ladder and tape the ladder to your bedroom door.

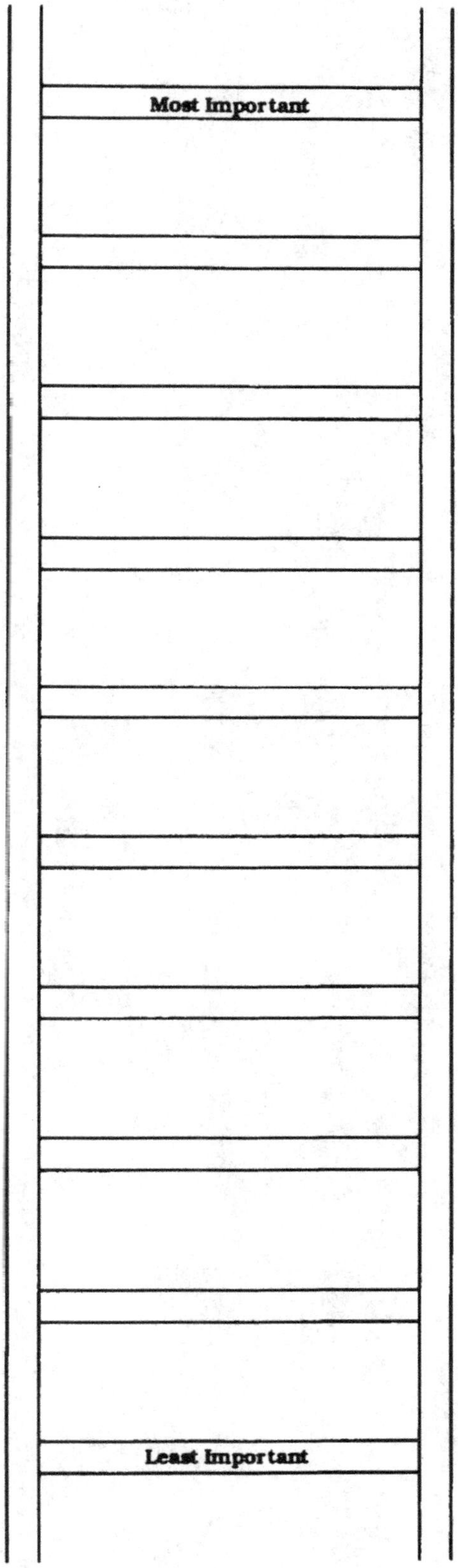

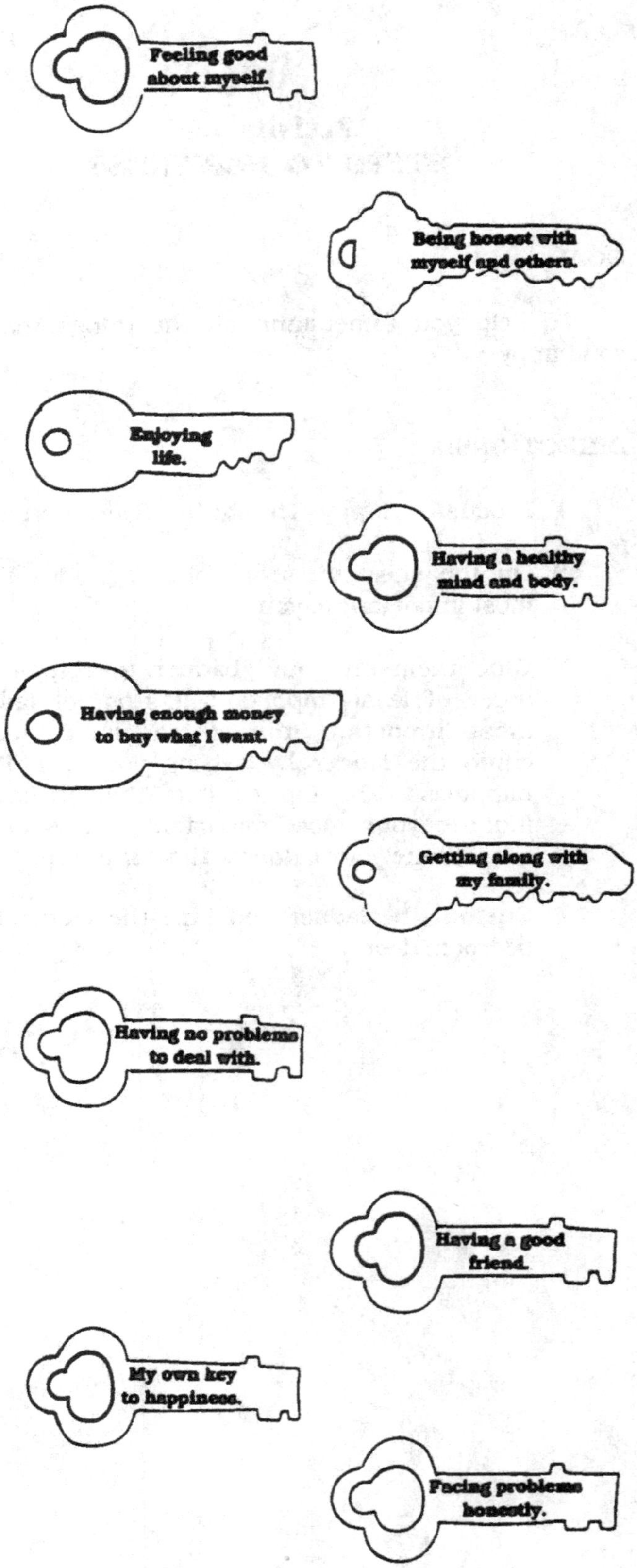
Feeling good about myself.
Being honest with myself and others.
Enjoying life.
Having a healthy mind and body.
Having enough money to buy what I want.
Getting along with my family.
Having no problems to deal with.
Having a good friend.
My own key to happiness.
Facing problems honestly.

Name ______________________________

Date ______________ Hour ______________

Activity 4.10
ASSESSING THE FEELING OF SADNESS.

GOAL:

To help you understand the feeling of sadness.

DIRECTIONS:

1. Fill out the "Causes for Sadness" sheet.

2. Complete the "Sadness Causes—Ones I can and can't control" sheet.

3. Complete "Ranking Sad Feelings" sheet.

HOMEWORK:

1. Ask three people what makes them sad. Ask the same three people what they allow to make them happy.

2. Record your answers on the "People's Sad and Happiness" sheet.

3. Summarize the results and bring them to class.

CAUSES FOR SADNESS

Sadness is a choice. You allow yourself to feel sad. Some situations in which you allow yourself to feel sad are

1. ______________________________

2. ______________________________

3. ______________________________

4. ______________________________

5. ______________________________

Name ______________________________

Date ____________ Hour ____________

SADNESS CAUSES
ONES I CAN AND CAN'T CONTROL

Some things in our lives that we feel sad about we have no control over. For example, we cannot control an airplane that crashes, an earthquake, or a flood. There are some things in our lives that we feel sad about which we can control. For example, if we let one of our friends down or didn't do something our parents wanted us to do, we choose to feel sad or guilty.

After a plane crash, an earthquake, a flood or letting our friend down or not doing something for our parents, we might feel sad. We cannot control a plane crash, an earthquake, or a flood but we can control our sad and guilty feelings about our friend and parents.

Put the things listed in the umbrella into either the section "Things I Can Control" or "Things I Cannot Control". You might want to add a few of your own ideas.

Things I Control

____

____

____

____

____

Things I Cannot Control

____

____

____

____

____

RANKING SAD FEELINGS

We can rank our sad feelings from least sad to most sad. There are some situations listed below that often make people feel sad. Put them in order so that the situation that feels most sad is at the top of the list and the situation that you feel the least sad about is at the bottom of the list. You might add any situations that have been left out.

Disagreement with a friend	1. ______________________
Loss of favorite possession	2. ______________________
My best friend moved to another state	3. ______________________
Grounding for not cleaning room	4. ______________________
Pet ran away	5. ______________________
Broken arm	6. ______________________
Not invited to a friend's party	7. ______________________
Parents not getting along	8. ______________________
Teacher yelling	9. ______________________
Not the right clothes to wear to school	10. ______________________
Someone calling you a name	11. ______________________
Not understanding the teacher	12. ______________________
Chosen last to be on the team in gym	13. ______________________
Low grade on test	14. ______________________

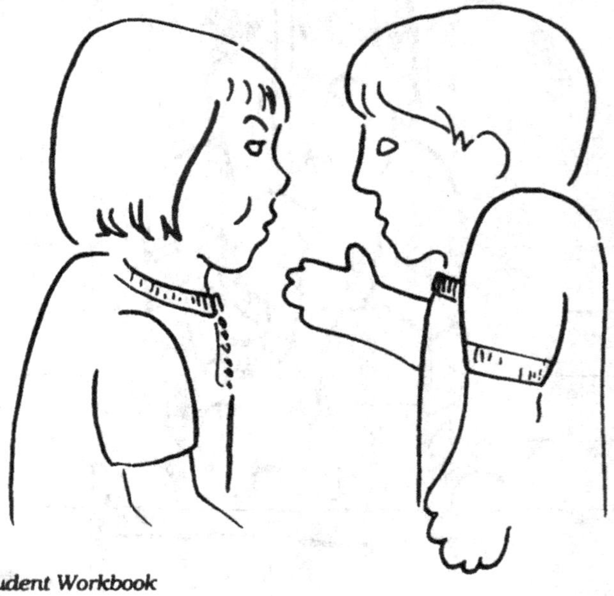

Name ______________________________

Date ____________ Hour ____________

PEOPLE'S SADNESS AND HAPPINESS

I am sad when . . . . .

____

____

____

I am happy when . . . . .

____

____

____

Make a summary of your poll.

____

____

____

____

____

____

____

____

Activity 4.11
SOLUTIONS FOR COPING WITH MY SADNESS

GOAL:

To learn solutions for coping with sadness.

DIRECTIONS:

1. Discuss with your leader examples of how you choose to be sad or glad.
2. Discuss ways you deal with sadness.
3. Mark with "X" what you like to do when you feel sad:

____ talk to a family member.

____ talk to a friend.

____ be alone in my room.

____ go to a quiet spot outdoors.

____ do some physical activity.

____ other ____

____

Name ______________________________

Date ____________ Hour ____________

4. Indicate how *you would like* to cope differently.

5. Write a paragraph on how you can change from what you are doing (answer to Item 3) to what you would like to do (answer to Item 4) regarding behavior relating to sadness.

____

____

____

____

____

HOMEWORK:

Practice your answers to Items 4 and 5.

Activity 4.12
LEARNING TO READ PEOPLE'S SAD EXPRESSIONS

GOAL:

To assist you in reading the faces of people and what they mean.

DIRECTIONS:

1. Recognize that facial expressions communicate feeling without using words.

2. Label the faces as to facial expressions using the terms below. Work with a partner.

   a. Frown
   b. Snarl
   c. Pout
   d. Scowl
   e. Sneer

3. Use a mirror to practice making these expressions on your face.

4. Describe (write your answers) a time when a person might

   a. Frown ______________________________
   b. Snarl ______________________________
   c. Pout ______________________________
   d. Scowl ______________________________
   e. Sneer ______________________________

5. Share with the group.

Name ____________________

Date ____________ Hour ____________

Activity 4.13
EASING SADNESS IN SELF AND OTHERS

GOAL:

To plan how to ease the sadness in self and others.

DIRECTIONS:

1. List some things you do when you feel sad.

____

____

____

____

____

2. Think about a time you felt sad. What did you do when you felt this sadness? Share your experience by writing about it and sharing it with a partner in class.

____

____

____

____

____

3. Listen to your partner's experience of sadness.

____

____

____

____

____

4. List some reasons for sadness and what you can do to lessen sadness.

5. Think of ways to ease the sadness for others. Write these in the space provided.

Name ______________________________

Date ______________ Hour ______________

Activity 4.14
RECOGNIZING ANGER

GOAL:

To help you recognize your anger in yourself.

DIRECTIONS:

1. Listen to leader discuss anger and the story of "Empty Lizzie."
2. Fill out "Anger" sheet and discuss responses with your group.

ANGER

Name ____

Three things that I get angry about are

1. ____
2. ____
3. ____

Three things that people get angry at me about are

1. ____
2. ____
3. ____

Two negative things (bad) I do when I get angry are

1. ____
2. ____

Two positive (good) ways I act when I am angry are

1. ______________________________

2. ______________________________

A time I really lost my temper was. . .

____

____

____

____

A time I almost lost my temper but controlled myself was. . .

____

____

____

____

A time I stored up my anger and took it out on the wrong person. . . .

____

____

____

____

Positive ways I can handle my anger are

____

____

____

____

IT'S OKAY TO *FEEL* ANGRY. . .
IT'S *NOT* OKAY TO HURT SOMEONE ELSE!

Name ______________________________

Date ______________ Hour ______________

Activity 4.15
DEALING WITH ANGER

GOAL:

To help you understand different ways of dealing with anger.

DIRECTIONS:

1. Identify when you become angry with a friend. Circle the letter which is most nearly the response you gave:

   a. I immediately talk over the problem with my friend.

   b. I immediately express anger to my friend without listening to his/her side of the story.

   c. I express anger to another person who has nothing to do with the problem.

   d. I wait until my anger is gone and discuss the problem with the appropriate friend.

   e. I hold the anger in until it is gone and never discuss the issue with my friend.

   f. Another possible solution: I ______________________________

2. Consider how your response might differ for different situations.

3. Discuss with your group ways of coping with anger.

HOMEWORK:

1. Write a short paragraph about how you can deal with anger.

2. Give an example of how you have dealt with anger between the time when you did Activity 4.15 and start of Activity 4.16.

3. Submit your homework at the next meeting.

Name ______________________________

Date ____________ Hour ____________

Activity 4.16
LEARNING TO FACE FEARS

GOALS:

1. To help you learn more about your fears.
2. To help you learn to develop activities to overcome those fears.

DIRECTIONS:

1. Follow the directions given by your leader.
2. Discuss how to tell when someone is afraid and/or tries to cover it up.
3. Discuss steps to overcome a fear.
4. When the leader instructs, write seven things that you fear on the "What Makes Me Afraid" Worksheet. Mark as to whether each is a physical (P) or emotional (E) fear.
5. When the leader instructs, write one fear you would like to overcome and what you can do to overcome it.

____

____

____

____

____

____

____

____

____

____

____

WHAT MAKES ME AFRAID

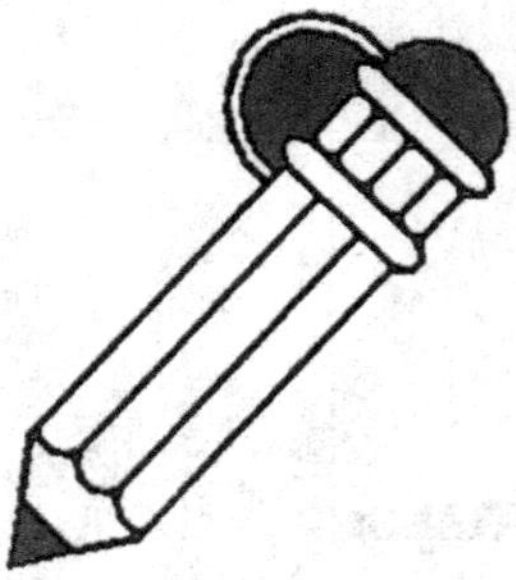

Write seven fears that you have. Then identify which are physical fears (P)—and which are emotional fears (E) such as fear of hurt feelings.

Mark P or E—Is this physical or emotional fear?

P or E

1. ______________________________

2. ______________________________

3. ______________________________

4. ______________________________

5. ______________________________

6. ______________________________

7. ______________________________

One fear I would like to overcome is ____________________

Something I can do about this fear is ____________________

Steps to overcome a fear:

1. Recognize it.
2. Share it.
3. Take action. These are some choices:
    a. Learn more about what you are afraid of.
    b. Try it.
    c. Avoid it.
    d. Ask for help.
    e. Let go of it—accept it.

Name ______________________________

Date ______________ Hour ______________

Activity 4.17
PUTTING MEANING AND FEELING RESPONSES TOGETHER

GOAL:

To learn to accurately hear feelings, meanings and both together.

DIRECTIONS:

1. Listening for the **meaning** of another is difficult because you must paraphrase what they mean but very briefly.

   Example—Boy: "I have been thinking about joining the scouts. My friends think that's for the birds. . . .they really give me a bad time. But I still want to join."

   You are saying: "that you really want to join scouts even if your friends give you a bad time."

   Practice with a partner sending a message and having them paraphrase meaning.

2. Listen for the **feelings** in the statement and respond with just feelings.

   Example—Peer says: "Here I go again. It is toward the end of the semester and I am way behind on my work, just barely passing. It is like I can't think ahead, one of my friends will come over and I don't want to do homework. Why can't I just say no to my friends and do my homework?"

   You say: "You feel frustrated."

   Practice with a partner by sending a message and your partner hearing just the feeling.

3. Try to put the two together (**meaning and feeling**) and respond to these. A good helper can hear both the meaning and feeling of a statement.

   Example—Peer: "I have been really looking forward to meeting the new boy. I have heard so much about him that I want to spend time with him."

   Response: "You feel excited about meeting the new boy in the class."

4. Divide into groups of three and one person play the helper, one the helpee, and one the observer. The helpee is to send at least one message and the helper gives one response with both feeling and meaning. The observer is to use the "Check Sheet on Helping" to record his or her observations during the role-play. The helper listens to the helpee for one statement and responds using the following format. You feel (feeling) ____

   ______________________ because (meaning) ______________________.

5. As observer, use the "Check Sheet on Helping" and the helper feedback.

CHECK SHEET ON HELPING

(For Use by Observer)

Circle the answer as you observe the helper.

1. The helper demonstrated **caring** (listening with the body) to the person being helped.
   a. a little
   b. some
   c. a lot
2. The helper **paraphrased** the feelings of the person being helped.
   a. a little
   b. some
   c. a lot
3. The helper heard both the **feeling** and the **meaning** of the person being helped.
   a. a little
   b. some
   c. a lot

MODULE 5
SENDING
"I"
MESSAGES
SKILLS

SENDING "I" MESSAGES SKILLS

At times, you will be upset by someone else's behavior. "I" messages will help you let the other person know that. There will also be times that you have been listening to another person and you have strong feelings about what they are saying so you may use an "I" message to share your feelings. This skill is very valuable as you try to be assertive with others.

Name ______________________________

Date _______________ Hour _______________

Activity 5.1
UNDERSTANDING ASSERTIVE, NONASSERTIVE, AND AGGRESSIVE COMMUNICATION

GOAL:

To help you learn the difference between assertive, nonassertive and aggressive communication.

DIRECTIONS:

1. Listen as your leader discusses the difference between assertiveness, nonassertiveness, and aggressiveness. Your leader will describe good and bad ways to ask for what you want.

2. Listen as your leader defines and gives examples as assertive, nonassertive, and aggressive characteristics.

3. Learn assertiveness skills which helps one to stand up effectively for one's own dignity, respect, and courtesy without putting others down, while at the same time helping others to state what they want. It involves the ability to express thoughts and feelings in an honest, straightforward fashion that shows respect for the other person. Assertive people feel good about themselves, are open and willing to take risks, and are responsible for their behavior.

   Assertive people

   a. have good eye contact,
   b. appear relaxed,
   c. appear calm,
   d. have facial expressions that are consistent with speech characteristics and content,
   e. talk in a strong firm voice, and
   f. are honest and direct.

   Assertive people also

   a. express feelings and beliefs honestly and directly,
   b. stand up for their legitimate rights,
   c. express respect and empathy for others,
   d. use "I" messages, and
   e. are often willing to select a solution from alternatives.

4. Learn about nonassertive behavior which is an ineffective way of communicating. Individuals who are generally nonassertive have difficulty expressing their opinions, beliefs, and feelings. They do not stand up for their rights and might feel as though they are taken advantage of by others. Nonassertive persons are not honest. They send two messages. Verbally they might say "That's O.K." while nonverbally they say "That's not O.K."

Nonassertive people

a. are shy,
b. are anxious and nervous,
c. put others ahead of themselves,
d. allow others to make decisions for them,
e. are not able to say no,
f. feel guilty if they say no, and
g. keep negative feelings inside.

Nonassertive people also are

a. always apologizing,
b. always making excuses,
c. silent, and
d. agreeing often with others.

5. Learn about aggressive behavior which is an ineffective way of communicating. People who are aggressive put others down and violate their rights. They believe the only way to communicate is to yell or cut someone down. Aggressive people try to humiliate, dominate, or put others down. They do not feel good about themselves.

Aggressive people

a. are hostile, sarcastic and blaming,
b. inappropriately try to be the person in charge at the expense of putting others down,
c. glare at others,
d. tighten their facial muscles, and
e. hold their bodies in an attacking or threatening posture (i.e., hands on hips, leaning forward, finger pointing).

Aggressive people also

a. use a loud tone of voice,
b. use "you" rather than "I" statements,
c. use sarcasm,
d. demands their own way, and
e. attack other's self-worth.

6. Reassemble into smaller groups when instructed to do so by your leader.

7. Model in your smaller group one of the three behaviors that your leader asks your smaller group to do.

8. Write what the aggressive behavior looked like to you.

____

____

9. Write how the aggressive behavior felt to you.

____

____

Name ______________________

Date ____________ Hour ____________

10. Write what the nonassertive behavior looked like to you.

____

____

11. Write how the nonassertive behavior felt to you.

____

____

12. Write what the assertive behavior looked like to you.

____

____

13. Write what the assertive behavior felt like to you.

____

____

14. Model as a group the following assertive behaviors:

a. stand or sit up straight in a relaxed manner;
b. look directly at the other person;
c. keep eye contact;
d. talk in a calm, full voice; and
e. be honest and direct.

15. Ròle-play the following situations when your leader asks you to do so:

a. A friend asks you to spend the night and you ask your parents.
b. You want to take some money out of your savings account to buy a new toy.
c. You want to stay out later than usual.
d. You want your brother to help you with your math problems.
e. You want an expensive pair of tennis shoes.
f. You want to go to the park and your friends don't.

HOMEWORK:

Record of My Assertive, Nonassertive, and Aggressive behaviors.

For the next week, keep a record of your behaviors.

1. Identify each behavior as assertive, nonassertive, or aggressive.

2. Briefly describe the behavior.

3. State your feelings at the time of each behavior.

4. Decide whether or not you believe the behavior was appropriate for the situation.

Date	Kind of Behavior	Brief Description of Behavior	Your Feeling At The Time	Appropriateness for Situation

If more space is needed, use plain paper and attach the paper to this workbook.

Be prepared to submit this sheet at the next meeting of your training group.

Name ______________________________

Date ______________ Hour ______________

Activity 5.2
UNDERSTANDING DIFFERENCES AMONG NONASSERTIVE, ASSERTIVE, AND AGGRESSIVE COMMUNICATION.

GOAL:

To learn to behave assertively.

DIRECTIONS:

1. Describe the looks of a nonassertive person. Dora Doormat is such a person.

____

____

____

2. When Dora Doormat asks for something, write an illustration of what she says.

____

____

____

3. Describe the looks of an aggressive person. Bully Bart is such a person.

____

____

____

4. When Bully Bart asks for something, write an illustration of what he says.

____

____

____

5. Describe the looks of an assertive person. Straight Sally is such a person.

____

____

____

6. When Straight Sally asks for something, write an illustration of how she asks straight out and says.

____

____

____

HOMEWORK:

For a week, observe people that look assertive, nonassertive, and aggressive. Describe why they appear to model these behaviors. Write your observations on the sheet entitled "Record of Observations of Others' Assertive, Nonassertive and Aggressive Appearances."

Record of Observations of Others' Assertive, Nonassertive, and Aggressive Appearances

For the next week keep a record of people you observe who appear to have assertive, nonassertive, and aggressive behavior.

Date	What Was Observed The Person's Appearance	Situation

Submit this "Record" at the next meeting.

Name ______________________________

Date ____________ Hour ____________

Activity 5.3
ASSERTIVE POSTURING

GOAL:

To learn how to be assertive by your tone of voice and body language.

DIRECTIONS:

1. Watch your leader demonstrate assertive body language.

2. Find a partner.

    a. Person A—use a firm voice and assertive body language and tell your partner "Yes, I want you to."

    b. Person B—use a firm voice and assertive body language and tell partner "No, I will not."

3. Reverse roles.

4. Discuss with the class and your leader how it felt to play each of the roles.

HOMEWORK:

On the next page, complete illustrations of Dora Doormat, Bully Bart, and Straight Sally.

1. Draw a stick figure of a nonassertive Dora Doormat when someone asks her to do something she doesn't want to do.

Dora Doormat

2. Draw Bully Bart when he is being aggressive.

Bully Bart

3. Draw Straight Sally while she is being assertive and saying "NO" straight out.

Straight Sally

Name ______________________

Date ____________ Hour ____________

Activity 5.4
SENDING "I" MESSAGES

GOAL:

To learn to be assertive using the "I" message.

DIRECTIONS:

1. Use the "I" message as a way to communicate in an assertive way. "I" messages also are helpful in getting out of conflict. Here are the parts of the "I" message:

"I" MESSAGE
I feel ______________________ when you ______________________ and I want you to ______________________________________

Example:

Situation:

My brother is making fun of the way I'm talking.

"I" Messages:

"I feel upset when you make fun of me and I want you to stop."

2. As your leader gives situations, give examples of "I" Messages.

3. Divide into groups of three. Your leader will give each group an index card with a situation written on it.

4. Read the situation for your group. One of the group members will respond to the situation using the "you" message and another member will use the "I" Message. The third member is an observer who shows what is seen and heard. Your group has five minutes to practice before your leader asks your group to act out your situation for the class.

HOMEWORK:

Practice writing the "I" message by completing the "I Statement Situations Worksheet." Your leader will help you with the first two. Then you complete the others as homework.

I STATEMENT SITUATIONS WORKSHEET

1. Your friend has been sulking and acting sad all day.

2. Your brother or sister is playing the stereo so loud it is interfering with your finishing your homework.

3. Your brother or sister borrows something and does not return it.

4. You are yelled at by a parent or teacher.

5. Your mom or dad spends an entire day with you doing things you want to do.

6. A friend keeps asking to copy your school work.

7. You have to do a speech in front of the class and someone is giggling.

8. Your mom and dad buy you a gift you have wanted for a long time.

9. Your brother or sister keeps getting into your things at home.

10. You have a fight with a friend over something she said about you.

Name ______________________

Date ____________ Hour ____________

Activity 5.5
PRACTICING "I" MESSAGES

GOAL:

To learn to send "I" messages.

DIRECTIONS:

1 Write a situation where you would like to be more assertive.

____

____

2. Review the "I" Message Model of Activity 5.4.

"I" MESSAGE
I feel ______________ when you ______________ and I want you to ______________________

3. Divide into groups of three and practice sending "I" messages with your own examples. One person plays the sender of "I" message. Another person plays the role of the person in the situation and the third person is to be the observer. The observer looks for the body behavior of the assertive person, how he or she sounded, and if the person gives a correct "I" message by completing the "I Message Observation Sheet." After each role-play, share and discuss what was heard and seen as reflected on the "I Message Observation Sheet."

4. In your role-play, switch and respond empathically to what the other person is doing or saying. Empathy responses were learned in Module 4.

Example:

Situation:

Your friend is calling you names
Student 1: Acts out situation
Student 2: Sends "I" message
Student 2: "I feel irritated when you call me names and I want you to be kinder to me."
Student 1, Response: "Well, you never pay attention to me when I make you mad."
Student 2: Respond empathically, "You are upset because I ignore you?"
Student 1: "Yes, I just want to talk to you at times."
Student 2: "Well, I will try to pay more attention to you in the future."
Student 1: "I will try to be kinder to you."

HELPFUL QUESTIONING SKILLS

At times when you listen to another person you might need to help the interaction along. Learning how to send effective questions will help facilitate the conversation. Questioning is also a good skill to use in groups as you lead small discussion groups.

Name ______________________________

Date ______________ Hour ______________

Activity 6.1
LEARNING ABOUT HELPFUL QUESTIONING

GOAL:

To learn more about questions that are helpful.

INFORMATION:

There are good questions and poor questions. They are known as open questions and closed questions.

Open questions cause us to talk more, for example, "Could you tell me more about your favorite sport?"

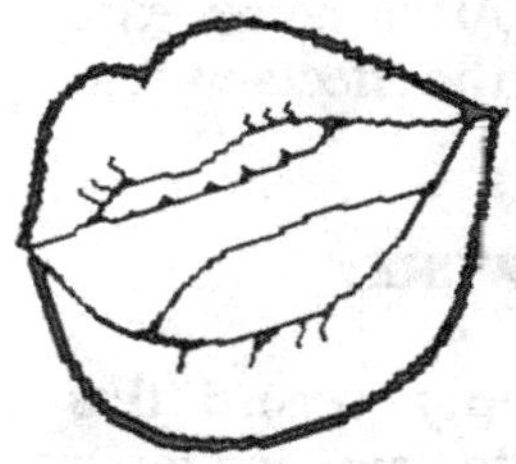

Closed questions tend to receive "yes" or "no" answers and often lead to stopping communication. For example, "Are you going to the movies Saturday afternoon?"

There are other kinds of questions, such as ones that make you feel bad and some that make you feel like others care. Some people can ask questions and its okay and others can ask questions and you feel irritated or scared.

DIRECTIONS:

1. Mark each of the following questions as to whether it is an open question or a closed question.

	Open	Closed
a. Given this information, what would you do?	______	______
b. Who was Lyndon Johnson?	______	______
c. Do you like milk?	______	______
d. Tell me about your feelings about school.	______	______
e. How do you show you are happy?	______	______
f. Tell me more about your problem with your brother.	______	______

2. After completing Item 1, discuss as a class the answers and why each is marked as it is.

3. Write two open questions.

   a. ______________________________

   b. ______________________________

4. Write two closed questions.

   a. ______________________________

   b. ______________________________

5. Rearrange yourselves into groups of two.

6. Practice with your partner asking each other questions written in Items 3 and 4.

7. After completing Item 4, discuss as a class what the effects were.

HOMEWORK:

Keep a record this next week of open questions and closed questions asked of you and write how each made you feel and/or behave.

Question	Check		How You Felt and/or Behaved
	Open	Closed	

Be prepared to submit your homework at the next meeting.

Name ______________________________

Date ______________ Hour ____________

Activity 6.2
OPEN QUESTIONS

GOAL:

To help you more fully understand the difference between open and closed questions.

DIRECTIONS:

1. Learn what open questions can do.

   a. Start a conversation.

      Example: "How do you feel about reading?"

   b. Tell more about the subject.

      Example: "Tell me more about how you feel about reading."

   c. Help understand the situation better.

      Example: "Give me examples of how reading is a problem for you."

   d. Help focus on feelings.

      Example: "How do you feel when you have difficulty reading?"

2. Learn what closed questions can do.

   a. Give just the facts.

      Example: "What grade did you make in reading?"

   b. Show that the helper is not really interested in the person.

      Example: "Why don't you practice reading every day to improve your grade?"

   c. Often stop communication.

      Example: "Why didn't you do better in reading?"

3. Discuss and give examples of open questions and closed questions with the leader and other group members.

4. Write an open question for each of the following two situations:

a. Your friend is having trouble with math. He looks upset.

Open question: ______________________________

b. Your neighbor tells you that she had a terrible experience.

Open question: ______________________________

5. Discuss the examples of open question in Item 4 with the class.

6. Identify three situations in which open questions would be helpful, tell why, and give example of an open question that might be appropriate for the situation.

Situation	Open Question Used	Outcome

7. Discuss as a group responses to Item 6.

HOMEWORK:

During the next 24 hours note the open questions you use, the different situations in which used, and the outcome (what you observed or heard)

Situation	Open Question Used	Outcome

Name ______________________

Date ____________ Hour ____________

Activity 6.3
PRACTICE OPEN QUESTIONING

GOAL:

To help you to practice open questioning in an interview.

DIRECTIONS:

1. Recognize the use of open questions in an interview:

   a. start an interview,
   b. keep the interview going,
   c. clarifying feelings, and
   d. learn more about the issue.

2. Review your skills of empathy (Module 4) and caring (Module 3) and how to use those skills in interviewing.

3. Form groups with three in each group.

4. Identify one person to play the role of the helper, one person to play the role of the helpee, and one person to be the observer.

5. As helpee, play the role of a person having a problem, such as problem with a friend, difficulty with a school subject, or a fight with an older brother or sister.

6. As helper, use open questions to bring out information, feelings, and general experiences and also to use attending and empathy skills while interviewing.

7. As observer, complete the "Observation Sheet" while the interview is being done and then share your feedback (observations and what you heard) after the interview ends.

8. Change roles, use a different situation, and repeat Items 5, 6, and 7.

9. Change roles again and repeat so that each person has each of the three roles.

10. Discuss as a group what occurred in your groups when role-playing.

OBSERVATION SHEET

DIRECTIONS: Mark (X) as you observe.

	YES	NO
1. Open questions were used to		
a. Start conversation	❐	❐
b. Keep the interview going	❐	❐
c. Clarify feelings	❐	❐
d. Learn more about the subject	❐	❐
2. Empathy:		
a. Put feelings into words	❐	❐
b. Put content into words	❐	❐
3. Caring:		
a. Looked interested in person talking	❐	❐
b. Used appropriate behaviors	❐	❐

HOMEWORK:

1. Watch for a time when you possibly can help someone by talking with him or her.
2. During your interview (talk), use open questions, caring skills, and empathy skills.
3. Write an account of your interview.

____

____

____

____

____

____

4. Be prepared to submit your homework at the next meeting.

MODULE 7
CONFLICT RESOLVING SKILLS

CONFLICT RESOLVING SKILLS

At times you may disagree with a friend or family member. Often these disagreements turn into fights. This is called conflict. The skills you will learn in this module will help you solve situations in a positive way. Also at times when you are on the playground or in the lunch room, you might listen to others in conflict. These skills will help you prevent or solve conflicts of others.

Name ______________________

Date ____________ Hour ____________

Activity 7.1
INTRODUCTION TO SOLVING CONFLICT

GOAL:

To learn the importance of solving conflicts effectively.

DIRECTIONS:

1. Think about the word "conflict." What does it mean to you?
2. Think of various situations in which conflict occurs. Listen as your leader discusses the impossibility of avoiding conflict and means of dealing with conflict.
3. Think of some conflict situations most common to you.
4. Tell your leader the way you might handle conflict as your leader categorizes them on the board.
5. Discuss with your leader and the class the concept of winners and losers in conflicts.
6. Take a look at the "Conflict: My Actions and Feelings." Complete the worksheet when your leader asks you to do so.
7. Decide of the categories your leader wrote on the board which raised the most serious conflict issues for you from your worksheet.
8. Submit your "Conflict: My Actions and Feelings" to your leader.

HOMEWORK:

1. Decide what goals you need to set for yourself about solving conflicts.

2. Think of situations in which you could improve and write them here.

____

____

____

____

____

3. Think about another student who needs help with conflict. With what kind of conflict does this person get involved?

____

____

4. Complete the following statements concerning conflict.

   a. My goal: ________________________________

   ____

   ____

   ____

   b. Where I need to improve: ________________________

   ____

   ____

   ____

   c. Someone I know has a conflict situation and the way I might assist positively is

   ____

   ____

   ____

   ____

5. Be prepared to submit the "Conflict: My Actions and Feelings" and the homework at the next meeting.

Name ______________________________

Date ______________ Hour ______________

CONFLICT: MY ACTIONS AND FEELINGS

Answer each question as honestly as you can. After experiencing conflict, describe your feelings in the last column. The purpose of this exercise is to see how you handle conflict situations.

	CONFLICT SITUATION	WHAT I USUALLY DO	HOW I FEEL
1	When someone calls me a name . . .		
2	When someone says it's my fault when it isn't . . .		
3	When I get pushed in line . . .		
4	When someone yells at me . . .		
5	When someone tries to get me to fight . . .		
6	When someone tries to talk me into doing something I don't want to do . . .		
7	When someone talks behind my back and lies about me . . .		

WRITE "A" IF YOU AGREE OR "D" IF YOU DISAGREE WITH THE STATEMENTS BELOW.

____ As long as there are people there will be conflict.

____ A conflict can be as small as an argument or as large as a war.

____ In a conflict there will always be a winner and a loser.

____ Conflicts between individuals or nations can sometimes be resolved in ways other than violence and war.

When I get angry I ____

I am __________ am not __________ satisfied with the way I now solve conflicts.

I would __________ would not __________ like to learn ways to solve conflicts.

Activity 7.2
GETTING ATTENTION

GOAL:

1. To learn positive ways to get attention.
2. To better understand how negative ways of obtaining attention often lead to conflict.

DIRECTIONS:

1. Define "attention" and discuss this with the class.
2. Think about how you get attention from others.
3. Mark by circling the number in the "Attention Checklist" the amount of attention you receive from those listed and the amount of attention you need from others.

ATTENTION CHECKLIST

	Very Low	Low	Medium	High	Very High
a. From your parents	1	2	3	4	5
your friends	1	2	3	4	5
your teachers	1	2	3	4	5
other students	1	2	3	4	5
relatives	1	2	3	4	5
b. The amount of attention you need from others	1	2	3	4	5

4. Discuss both positive and negative ways to get attention. Your leader will write class suggestion on the board.
5. Write three ways that you get attention in a positive manner.

a. ______________________________

____

b. ______________________________

____

c. ______________________________

____

Name ______________________________

Date ______________ Hour ____________

6. Write three ways that you get attention in a negative manner.

   a. ______________________________

   b. ______________________________

   c. ______________________________

7. With your leader's directions, discuss how negative attention often leads to conflict.

8. Write how satisfied you are with attention:

   a. you receive from others. ______________________________

   b. you give to others. ______________________________

9. Brainstorm positive ways to give and receive attention. These are additional ways to those listed in Item 4.

10. Write what you would like to change:

    a. in how you receive or obtain attention from others. ______________________________

    b. in how you give attention to others. ______________________________

HOMEWORK:

In the space below, write a personal goal to obtain attention in a positive way. Be as specific as you can.

1. Goal

   Example: To have Mom express appreciation to me.

   My Goal: ____

   ____

   ____

   ____

   ____

   ____

   ____

   ____

2. Behavior on your part to achieve the goal.

   Example: I will clean and straighten up my room and leave the door open so that Mom can see what I did.

   My behavior will be ____

   ____

   ____

   ____

   ____

   ____

   ____

   ____

3. Be prepared to submit your homework at the next meeting.

Name ______________________

Date ____________ Hour ____________

Activity 7.3
WHAT ROLE ARE YOU?

GOAL:

To see the importance of roles in cooperating with one another.

DIRECTIONS:

1. Listen carefully as your leader introduces activities to be completed in your group. Your leader will award points according to how much of the activity your group completes.

2. When time is up at the first task or station, move to the next station. Repeat until your small group has worked at the task at each station.

3. After completing all the tasks (Item 2), complete the following.

COOPERATION AND ROLES QUESTIONNAIRE

a. Who was the leader of your group?

b. Why was that person the leader?

c. Were there any observers or nonparticipants in your group?

d. Did your group have a rebel, or a person that always challenged the leader's decisions?

e. How did the leader help with the group's decisions?

4. Think about the importance of cooperating. How big a role did cooperation play when your group worked at each station your leader assigned? Write your observations in the space below.

____

____

____

____

____

5. Discuss in the total group your answers to Items 3 and 4.

6. Discuss in the total group different roles people often have or take when they are with other people, for examples, follower, leader, observer, helper, clown, loner, and rebel.

7. Discuss, as a class, how these experiences in this Activity 7.3 relate to everyday life.

HOMEWORK:

1. Complete the "Roles" sheet in the Workbook.

2. Be prepared to submit the homework at the next meeting.

ROLES

The circle represents all of the time you spend with other people. How much of the time are you a follower? A leader? An observer? A helper? A clown? A loner? A rebel? Divide the circle into wedges like a pie and label the parts.

Parts:

a. follower

b. leader

c. observer

d. helper

e. clown

f. loner

g. rebel

h. other (specify) ____________________

____

____

Name ______________________

Date ____________ Hour ____________

Activity 7.4
THE SEESAW GAME

GOAL:

To help you understand that conflict goes nowhere and that a person controls conflict by walking away.

DIRECTIONS:

1. Listen as your leader defines a seesaw.

2. Keep in mind that this activity is only to show you to walk away from conflict. Brainstorm with the class some general harmful comments you have made or have been made to you.

3. Watch as your leader asks two students to demonstrate how the seesaw works.

4. Observe what happens when one of the demonstrators walks away from the seesaw.

5. Discuss with your leader and the class who wins the seesaw game and how you can do things to prevent the seesaw game in your relationships with others.

HOMEWORK:

1. Turn to the "Tug-of-War Activity" sheet in your workbook. Complete this sheet after thinking about situations where you feel one person is tugging one end while you are tugging the other end.

2. During this next week, complete the following:

Situation Noticed Where People Were in Conflict	How Did the Conflict Stop? Results?	Record Your Feelings About This Event

3. If you can conveniently do so, bring a tape recorder and a blank tape to the next class session.

4. Be prepared to submit your homework at the next meeting.

TUG-OF-WAR ACTIVITY

WHAT MAKES YOU FIGHT BACK-AND-FORTH WITH ANOTHER PERSON? LOOK AT THE TWO SAD FACES ACROSS FROM THE ARROW. WRITE WHAT THEY MIGHT BE ARGUING ABOUT IN THE SPACE BELOW THE DRAWING.

____

____

____

____

What feelings do you have when you are in a tug-of-war? ______________________________

____

How does it feel when you win? ______________________________

____

How does it feel when you lose? ______________________________

____

Can you think of anything you could do differently? If so, write your ideas below. ____________

____

Name ______________________________

Date ____________ Hour ____________

Activity 7.5
RELAXATION AND IMAGERY EXPERIENCE

GOAL:

To learn deep relaxation and imagery experience.

DIRECTIONS:

1. Listen as your leader explains and demonstrates the difference between tension and relaxation.

2. Listen as your leader explains that imagery is used to help people improve in many ways.

3. Listen carefully, your leader will explain that relaxation and imagery go together.

4. Listen to your leader as you are given instructions for a relaxation and imagery experience.

5. Write your comments about the experience.

____

____

____

____

6. Discuss your reactions of your experience.

HOMEWORK:

1. Practice everyday this next week the relaxation and imagery activity. use your tape if you make one during Activty 7.5.

2. After a couple of days of practice, recall a conflict situation and try to use the relaxation and imagery activity to resolve it. Then in the Workbook complete two pages. One is entitled "Draw a Picture of Yourself in a Conflict Resolution" and the other is entitled "Draw a Picture of Yourself Relaxed and Dealing with Conflict Resolution."

3. Before the next class session, complete the page in the Workbook entitled "Comments Related to Image Experiences."

4. Be prepared to submit your homework at the next meeting.

DRAW A PICTURE OF YOURSELF IN A CONFLICT RESOLUTION

How strong was the image? ____

____

____

How clear was the image? ____

____

____

Name ______________________________

Date ______________ Hour ______________

DRAW A PICTURE OF YOURSELF RELAXED AND DEALING WITH CONFLICT RESOLUTION

How strong was the image? ____

____

____

How clear was the image? ____

____

____

COMMENTS RELATED TO IMAGE EXPERIENCES

1. How tense did you feel before the relaxation and imagery experience? ______________________

____

____

2. What situation did your first image reflect? ______________________

____

____

3. How did you feel as you drew your second image? ______________________

____

____

4. How did you look in the second image? ______________________

____

____

5. How did you sound in your second image? ______________________

____

____

6. Record events during the week where you were able to use your imagination to relax as you were dealing with a conflict.

Name ______________________________

Date ______________ Hour ______________

Activity 7.6
CHANGING NEGATIVE THOUGHTS INTO POSITIVES

GOAL:

To learn that one of the keys of developing self-esteem and reducing conflict is to talk positively to oneself.

DIRECTIONS:

1. Discuss with the group and your leader what self-esteem is and what differences are between high and low self-esteem.
2. Look at pictures presented by your leader and identify those with high self-esteem and those with low self-esteem.
3. Discuss the kinds of messages said when people feel good about themselves compared to messages said when people feel bad about themselves.
4. Complete the page in the Workbook entitled "Self-talk."
5. After completing the "Self-talk" sheet, discuss with the class.

HOMEWORK:

During this next week record those times when you experienced very positive self-esteem and those times when you experienced very negative self-esteem. Complete the sheet on "Self-esteem and Self-talk."

SELF-ESTEEM AND SELF-TALK

Situations When I Had Very Positive Self-esteem	Self-talk During the Situation

Situations When I Had Negative Self-esteem	Self-talk During the Situation

Name ______________________

Date ____________ Hour ____________

SELF-TALK

List some sentences that the happy-faced person is saying inside.

1. ____
____
2. ____
____
3. ____
____

List some sentences that the sad-faced person is saying inside.

1. ____
____
2. ____
____
3. ____
____

Activity 7.7
CANCELLING NEGATIVE THOUGHTS

GOAL:

To learn to cancel negative thoughts.

DIRECTIONS:

1. Look at the picture your leader has of a person who is feeling down. Discuss what that person thinks of himself or herself.

2. Discuss with your leader what "cancel" means.

3. Listen as your leader explains how cancelling is a way to combat poor self-esteem.

4. Listen as your leader explains how to combat negative thinking. Write the process in the spaces below.

   a. ______________________________

   b. ______________________________

   c. ______________________________

5. Review the above process by role-playing with the class.

6. Review with your leader the following on inner-voices:

INNER-VOICES

JEAN: Yo, Dana. How are you doing?

JEAN'S INNER VOICE: I'm glad I found someone to talk to.

DANA: I'm okay.

DANA'S INNER VOICE: I'm surprised Jean talked to me. I didn't think she liked me!

JEAN: We sure had a tough run in gym today.

JEAN'S INNER VOICE: I'm running farther and faster than I used to. I might get pretty good if I keep improving!

DANA: Yeah. I hate running.

DANA'S INNER VOICE: I'm never going to be any good at running. It's too hard.

Name ______________________________

Date ______________ Hour ______________

HOMEWORK:

1. Look at the page entitle "Cancel Negatives."

2. Think about a time when you gave yourself a negative message. Write about that time on the worksheet.

3. What did you think about during those times?

4. Remember to use the "cancel" sign or "stop" sign when you start to think negatively.

5. Write out a thought on your worksheet that will help you do your best.

6. Be prepared to share your positive thoughts with the group at the next session.

CANCEL NEGATIVES

1. Tell about a time when you gave yourself a negative message.

2. What do you think to yourself at these times?

3. Learn to ask yourself if this thought is helping you to do your best. If the answer is "NO" then **CANCEL!!**

4. Write out a thought that will help you to do your best.

Name ______________________

Date ____________ Hour ____________

Activity 7.8
CONFLICT STOPPERS

GOAL:

To learn a number of ways to avoid or stop conflict.

DIRECTIONS:

1. Study the Four-Step Conflict Stoppers. Notice that the ideas of solving conflict are grouped under four simple steps. Some of these are ideas that you have already learned about in your peer helper training.

FOUR-STEP CONFLICT STOPPERS

1. STOP

Spot Conflict

Decide to Get Involved

2. LOOK

Stay Relaxed

Send Positive Message to Self

3. LISTEN

Use Empathy

Give "I" Message

Give New Idea

4. THEN ACT

Get Adult Help

2. Discuss in the class session the meanings of each of the four steps.

3. On the card the leader will give you, write a conflict situation that has happened to you.

4. Regroup into small groups of three and then role-play your conflict.

   a. First, practice it with another member of your group entering into the conflict. The third member will observe and give feedback afterwards.

   b. Second, practice it using the "Four-Step Conflict Stoppers."

   c. Rotate so that each of you in your group has an opportunity to role-play his or her conflict as written on the card.

5. Perform one of your role-plays in front of the class and discuss these as directed by your leader.

   a. What error did the person make that got him or her into the conflict situation?

   b. How did the group handle the conflict?

   c. What other ideas might have been helpful to resolve the conflict?

6. Discuss ways as a group that you have learned to avoid conflict.

7. For a goal for yourself, write in the space below steps you will follow to avoid conflict.

____

____

____

____

____

____

____

____

HOMEWORK

1. On the sheet entitled "Getting Along with Others," write your responses for the four cases.

2. Be prepared to sumbit your homework at the next meeting.

Name ______________________________

Date ______________ Hour ______________

GETTING ALONG WITH OTHERS

CASE 1

John was standing in line waiting to go to lunch. Another student, named Jack, crowded in front of John and said, "Get out of the way. This is my place, not yours?" What should John do to avoid conflict?

CASE 2

Lisa was Mary's sister. When they got home after school, Lisa would turn her stereo up as loud as it would go. This was really bothering Mary. What should she do to avoid conflict?

CASE 3

Wayne and Doug were playing outside at recess. Doug turned toward Wayne and called him a bad name. He then started asking Wayne to fight. He kept calling him a "chicken" and a "dork." Wayne is really mad and upset about this and is ready to fight. What should he do to avoid conflict?

CASE 4

Joy was a popular girl in school. She was liked by most of her classmates. One day she was told by another girl that Kate was spreading rumors about her that were not true. Joy found Kate and several girls whispering in the lunchroom and looking over at her and laughing. Joy was very upset. The girls started to walk toward her pointing and laughing. What should Joy do to avoid conflict?

MODULE 8
DECISION-MAKING AND GOAL-SETTING SKILLS

DECISION-MAKING AND GOAL-SETTING SKILLS

Decision making can be hard to do. Often we must consider what is important to us, what we value, what others think, and finally what we can do. After making a decision, then we must put those decisions into practice.

Name ______________________

Date ____________ Hour ____________

Activity 8.1
MAKING DECISIONS WITH CLAY

GOALS:

1. To work with the clay and have fun with it.
2. To learn that decisions are involved even in leisure situations.

DIRECTIONS:

1. Observe and follow the three rules your leader writes on the board.
2. Wait as your leader passes out the clay.
3. Make whatever you wish out of the clay provided or enjoy it at your desk in whatever way you wish.
4. Share your creation with the class.
5. Mold the clay into a ball and return it as directed by your leader.
6. As your leader picks up the clay, write answers to all of the following questions:
   a. How difficult was it to decide what to do with the clay?

   ____

   ____

   ____

   b. Did you feel you had to have a finished product?

   ____

   ____

   ____

   c. What decisions were involved in working with the clay?

   ____

   ____

   ____

7. Discuss as a group the topics raised by your leader.

Activity 8.2
A FIXED CHOICE GAME

GOALS:

1. To help you look at how you and others make choices.

2. To experience choice making when no right or wrong answer exists.

DIRECTIONS:

1. Listen as your leader instructs you on how to play this game.

2. Have fun doing the things your leader asks you to do in the game.

3. After completing the game, write answers to the following:

   a. What were some of your feelings about your decisions?

   ____

   ____

   b. What did you learn about how others in the group made decisions?

   ____

   ____

   c. What did you learn about yourself about how you make decisions?

   ____

   ____

4. Discuss in the group answers to questions in Item 3.

5. Think about the risk taking you felt when making the decisions and discuss these in the group.

6. Discuss the role of your personal goals and values in decision making.

Name ______________________________

Date ______________ Hour ______________

Activity 8.3
DECISION POINT

GOAL:

To help you understand decision making as choices between two or more things.

DIRECTIONS:

1. Listen as your leader explains that the decision point occurs when you make a choice between two or more things.

2. Brainstorm (quickly recall) decisions you have made today. (What to have for breakfast? What to wear?)

3. Think about and discuss in the group the following:

   a. Are some decisions made for you?

   ____

   ____

   b. Which ones?

   ____

   ____

   c. By whom?

   ____

   ____

   d. Why must some decisions be made for us by others?

   ____

   ____

4. Think about how you make decisions, such as habits, likes, dislikes, and pressure from others, and notice how you make the decisions as your leader gives you some things to do.

5. Discuss within the group how you made your decisions and what things entered into the process.

Name ______________________________

Date ______________ Hour ______________

Activity 8.4
PREDICTING CONSEQUENCES

GOAL:

To help you understand that actions often have consequences.

DIRECTIONS:

1. Listen as your leader explains the importance of predicting consequences.
2. List all the consequences you can for each of the following decisions. Then label each consequence as good or bad.

	Good	Bad
a. Your family decided not to have a telephone. Consequences ______________________________ ______________________________ ______________________________	________	________
b. The grocery store owner in your neighborhood decided to close the store. Consequences ______________________________ ______________________________ ______________________________	________	________
c. The firefighters decided not to come to a fire. Consequences ______________________________ ______________________________ ______________________________	________	________

	Good	Bad
d. The teachers decided to stop teaching. Consequences ______________________________ ______________________________	______	______
e. The children decided not to come to school anymore. Consequences ______________________________ ______________________________	______	______
f. Gas stations decided not to sell any more gasoline. Consequences ______________________________ ______________________________	______	______
g. The children in your class decided to leave all their supplies out instead of putting them away. Consequences ______________________________ ______________________________	______	______
h. The city decided to make a new park in the neighborhood near your home. Consequences ______________________________ ______________________________	______	______

3. Discuss as a group answers to each part of Item 2 and, as you do, note how looking at consequences can help in making decisions.

4. Write what you have learned about thinking about and listing possible consequences before making decisions.

____

____

____

____

____

____

____

Name ______________________________

Date ______________ Hour ______________

Activity 8.5
CHOICES

GOAL:

To help you understand your values.

DIRECTIONS:

1. Define value and enter into the discussion as your leader asks you to do so.
2. Think about and write how your values affect your choices.
3. Complete the sheet in the Workbook, entitled "What Do I Value?"
4. After completing Item 3, move into smaller groups as directed by your leader.
5. Discuss in your small group the reason(s) behind your choice. Notice the differences in reasons among members of your group even when the choices are similar.
6. Discuss the items your leader will ask you to consider.

HOMEWORK:

Before the next group meeting, please complete the following:

1. Write a real life situation which required you to make a choice.

   ____

   ____

2. List some values that you hold that affected your choice.

   ____

   ____

3. Identify some of the positive consequences that might occur from your decision.

   ____

   ____

4. Identify some of the negative consequences that might occur from your decision.

   ____

   ____

5. Be prepared to submit your homework at the next meeting.

WHAT DO I VALUE?

DIRECTIONS:

1. Select from this list the three that you value most. Place a "M" before those three.
2. Next, select from this list the three that you value least. Place a "L" before those three.
3. Then write what you learned about yourself.

Three Valued Most	Three Valued Least	Things
____	____	Honesty
____	____	Financial Security (Enough money to live comfortably)
____	____	An exciting life (A fun, active life)
____	____	A world of peace (A world free from wars and fighting)
____	____	Health (Having good physical and emotional health)
____	____	Religion (Having religious beliefs)
____	____	Self-respect (Respecting and liking yourself)
____	____	Loyal friendship (having close friends and being loyal to them)
____	____	Intelligence (Being smart, educated)
____	____	Family togetherness (Being part of a family)
____	____	A world of equality (Equal rights for everyone)
____	____	Trust
____	____	Responsibility
____	____	Other ____________________

I learned . . .

____

____

Name ______________________

Date ____________ Hour ____________

Activity 8.6
FINDING WORDS TO EXPRESS VALUE

GOAL:

To help you understand some of the words that are values.

DIRECTIONS:

1. Complete the sheet entitled "Finding Words to Express Value."

2. After completing the puzzle, think of other words that represent values and write them below.

   ____
   ____
   ____
   ____
   ____
   ____
   ____

3. If time permits, use the words you wrote in Direction No. 2 and make a puzzle like the one with which you worked in Direction No. 1.

   ____
   ____
   ____
   ____
   ____
   ____
   ____

FINDING WORDS TO EXPRESS VALUE

DIRECTIONS:

Some words in the box below will tell you some good qualities for boys and girls to have in school and at home. The words are mixed in with all the letters you see in the box. You can find the words sometimes in a row of letters that goes forward or backward or in a row that goes up and down. Some words might go in a diagonal line. Draw a circle around each word as you find it. The words listed at the bottom are the ones for which you are looking.

A	G	E	D	N	S	R	K	W	H	I	M	B	U	H
R	L	U	F	T	S	U	R	T	O	D	Q	P	L	L
S	O	P	R	S	H	E	L	P	F	U	L	Z	I	O
B	L	S	T	H	O	U	G	H	T	F	U	L	Y	Y
K	U	I	C	D	X	A	L	E	L	W	O	C	P	A
N	F	N	B	E	Y	B	E	A	R	Y	G	L	Q	L
S	H	C	N	E	A	T	T	R	U	T	H	F	U	L
I	T	E	H	I	N	D	R	A	G	G	O	R	D	I
E	I	R	K	C	H	O	N	E	S	T	O	A	R	D
L	A	E	I	R	Y	B	T	H	S	T	E	V	E	G
H	F	W	M	B	R	E	L	I	A	B	L	E	S	Z
G	O	O	D	Z	N	E	Y	W	P	L	Y	R	K	A
A	W	Y	L	D	N	E	I	R	F	L	I	G	I	N
Y	A	H	E	R	Z	S	Z	A	P	A	T	C	N	M
M	T	K	A	L	Q	B	O	H	F	P	S	E	D	U

List of words to find in the group of letters above:

honest
friendly
sincere
truthful
thoughtful
helpful
loyal
trustful
fair
kind
faithful
reliable
good

Name ______________________________

Date ______________ Hour ______________

Activity 8.7
MAKING DECISIONS

GOAL:

To help you understand that values influence decisions.

INTRODUCTION:

Everybody makes decisions daily. Some of the decisions are more important than others. Some are so important they require thought, study, and investigation before a decision is made, while others are "automatic."

DIRECTIONS:

1. Discuss with the leader and the group the idea of all people making decisions every day.
2. Complete the sheet entitled "Typical Decisions."
3. Discuss your feelings after completing Item 2.
4. From the sheet entitled "What Do I Value?" that you completed in Activity 8.5, take two of your three most valued and complete as shown in the example.

   Example: I value "health" very much.

   As a result I will be concerned about my decisions

   in what I eat,
   in cleanliness of food I eat,
   in exercise I get, and
   in smoking and in being around people who smoke a lot.

   a. I value ______________________________ very much.

   As a result I will be concerned about my decisioins

   ____

   ____

   b. I value ______________________________ very much.

   As a result I will be concerned about my decisions

   ____

   ____

TYPICAL DECISIONS

DIRECTIONS:

The following table lists decisions faced by many students daily. Read the list and consider how YOU would make each decision. Check the appropriate category. If an example is not appropriate for you, leave that one blank.

TYPICAL DECISION	CATEGORY	
	Automatic	Must Think About
1. To get up early or late in the morning	______	______
2. What to eat for breakfast	______	______
3. To lie	______	______
4. To criticize a friend behind his/her back or to his/her face	______	______
5. Whether or not to smoke	______	______
6. To perform an assigned job	______	______
7. What to read	______	______
8. To study or watch TV the night before a test	______	______
9. When to come home at night	______	______
10. To tattle on friends	______	______
11. To go to school	______	______
12. To go to church	______	______
13. What to do with trash	______	______
14. What to buy for a present	______	______
15. To save part of your allowance	______	______
16. At whose house to stay overnight	______	______
17. To wear make-up	______	______

Name ______________________

Date ____________ Hour ____________

Activity 8.8
DECISION MAKING

GOAL:

To help you learn a model for making decisions.

DIRECTIONS:

1. Discuss with your leader the "Five-Step Process" needed in decision making.

Five-Step Process

a. State the problem clearly. List the goals or objectives that are to be achieved.

b. Search for alternatives. List as many choices and alternatives as possible.

c. List the pros and cons for each alternative. Think about probable consequences for each alternative.

d. Choose the best alternative after weighing and analyzing the probable consequences for each alternative.

e. Check your decision out with a trusted adult.

2. Go through the examples below using the "Five-Step Process" for making decisions.

a. What clothes to wear.

b. Whether to talk to your friend on the playground before school or to study a little longer for the upcoming social studies test.

c. Whether to cheat on a test for which you are not prepared, or to do the best you can on your own.

d Whether to ride the bus home or walk with friends.

e. What to bring to school for lunch.

f. Whether to give your book report today or try to get out of it until tomorrow.

g. Whether to go to a friend's party Saturday night or go to a baseball game with Dad.

h. Whether or not to volunteer to show your report card to your parents or wait until they ask.

i. Whether or not to tell your friend some unpleasant gossip that you have heard.

j. Whether or not to share your cookies with a friend at lunch.

3. Listen to the story that your leader will read. Then go through the decision-making process.

   a. State Randy's problem clearly.

   ____

   ____

   ____

   b. State alternative actions for Randy.

   ____

   ____

   ____

   c. List pros and con (consequences) of each alternative.

   ____

   ____

   ____

   d. Choose the alternative that seems best.

   ____

   ____

   ____

   e. Select an adult to whom Randy can go to "check out" his decision.

   ____

   ____

   ____

Name ____________________

Date ____________ Hour ____________

Activity 8.9
RELATING VALUES TO DECISIONS

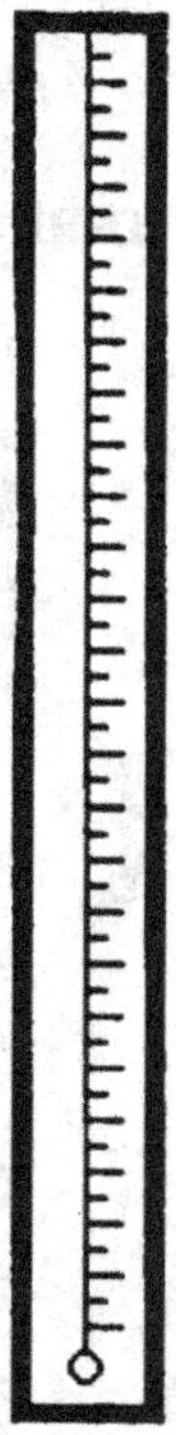

GOAL:

To help you understand what is behind your decisions.

DIRECTIONS:

1. Enter into a discussion with your leader and group members about understanding the "why" behind decisions.

2. Review definition of value that you wrote in your workbook Activity 8.5, Item 1, and modify if you have changed your concept (Write answer below).

 ____

 ____

 ____

3. Review values you identified in Activity 8.5 on the sheet entitled "What Do I Value?" Then list other values held.

 Values held: ______________________________

 ____

4. Write an important decision that you have made within the last year and identify what values you hold that helped you in making that decision.

 a. Decision I made: ______________________________

 ____

 b. My values that helped me make the decision: ______________________________

 ____

5. Share, if you feel comfortable doing so, your decision as written in Item 4a.

6. As decisions are shared, guess values that the person has that were important and might have been significant in the decision-making process.

Activity 8.10
RECOGNIZING GOALS AND RESPONSIBILITIES

GOAL:

To understand that goals have values behind them.

DIRECTIONS:

1. Define responsibility, and write your definition in the space below.

____

____

____

2. Define goals, and write that definition in the space below.

____

____

____

3. List two goals you have

   a. at school

      (1) ____

      ____

      (2) ____

      ____

   b. at home

      (1) ____

      ____

      (2) ____

      ____

4. Discuss with your leader and the group how you are responsible for the goals you listed in Item 3.

5. Discuss how others are dependent upon you in reaching your goal and how they value you as you achieve those goals.

Name ______________________________

Date ______________ Hour ____________

Activity 8.11
WISH UPON A STAR

GOAL:

To help you understand that once you set a goal, you will need to make decisions to help achieve the goal.

DIRECTIONS:

1. Brainstorm goals you would like to have come true within the next year.

2. Select the goal that is most important from those you brainstormed and write that important goal in the middle of the star in the workbook. An example is show where the goal is to "Make a good grade in Math."

3. Decide which values you have that are connected to the goal and place those values in the points of the star. See the example where values are "education, relationship among numbers, and feeling good about self."

4. Attach to the points of the star those decisions that possible will need to be made to help achieve the goal.

Model:

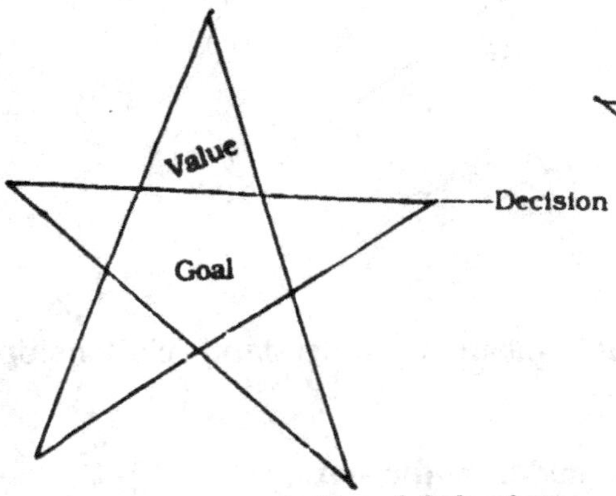

Example:

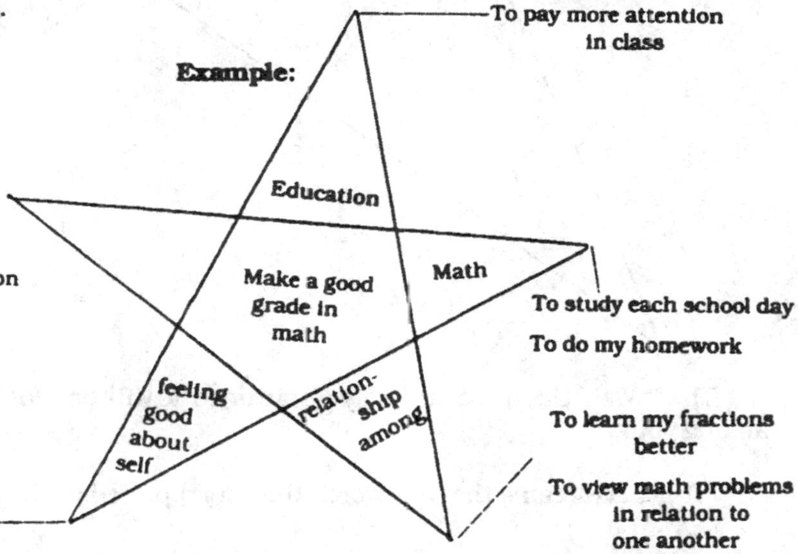

5. Write what steps you have taken this past week or will take this next week to help achieve the goal.

____

____

____

MY GOAL, RELATED VALUES, AND DECISIONS I HAVE MADE

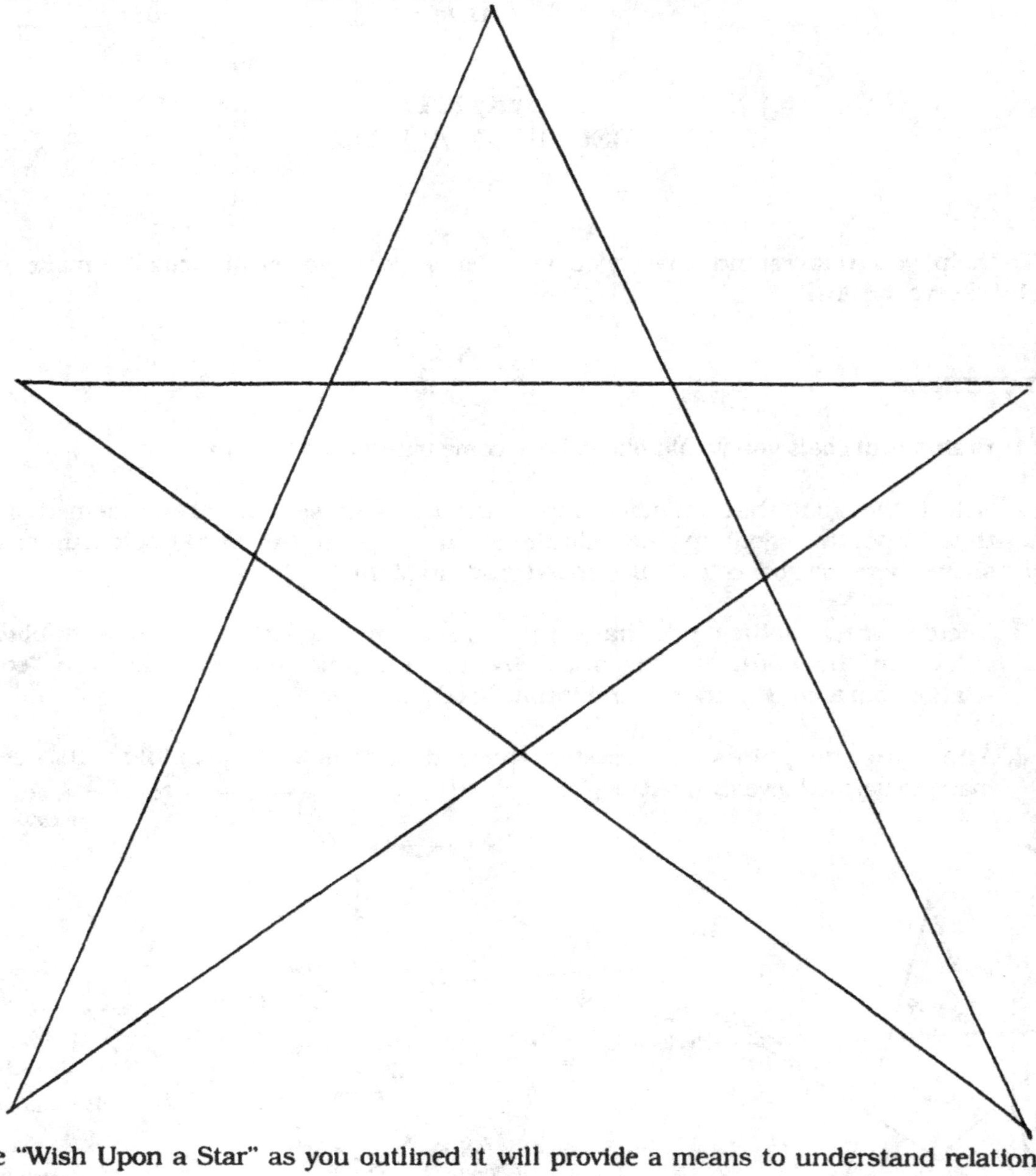

The "Wish Upon a Star" as you outlined it will provide a means to understand relationships among your

1. goals (dreams that are worth the effort) placed in the middle of the star.
2. values (ones you have or will need to acquire if your goal is to be achieved) in point,
3. decisions (ones that you possibly will need to make if you achieve your goal) attached to the point, and
4. steps, changes, or actions to be taken to fulfill each decision (Item 5 on previous page).

Name ______________________________

Date ______________ Hour ______________

Activity 8.12
ONCE UPON A TIME

GOALS:

1. To help you better understand the concept of change.

2. To help you better understand that changes might necessitate modifications in goals.

DIRECTIONS:

1. Think of the ways you've changed from yesterday to today, from last year to this year, and so forth.

2. Share with the group some of the changes you remembered in Item 1.

3. Write how you feel about change and then share with the group. Do you have a difficult time changing the way you act?

____

____

____

4. Write some experiences that have caused your changes.

   Examples:

   Had a new baby brother
   Moved to a new city
   Mother and Father got a divorce

____

____

____

5. Share how those experiences have caused you to change.

6. Write two or three most important changes that have occurred in your life so far.

____

____

____

7. Discuss how your changes in Item 6 have modified your goals over time.

8. Listen as your leader reads a poem about himself or herself. This is the same poem stem as the one you have in your homework.

HOMEWORK:

1. Complete the "Once, But Now" poem.

ONCE, BUT NOW

DIRECTIONS: Complete this poem and share it with your leader and members of your group. The poem need not rhyme. What you are needing to do is look at how things once were and then look at how they have changed to what they are now.

Once I felt ______________________________

But now I feel ______________________________

Once I though ______________________________

But now I'm sure ______________________________

Once I wondered ______________________________

But know I know ______________________________

Once I couldn't ______________________________

But now I can ______________________________

Once I was ______________________________

But now I am ______________________________

Once I wanted ______________________________

But now I have ______________________________

Once I wished for ______________________________

But now I wish ______________________________

2. Be prepared to share your poem with the group at the next meeting.

Name ______________________________

Date ____________ Hour ____________

Activity 8.13
MEMORY LINE

GOAL:

To help you visualize those changes that have taken place from one age to another.

DIRECTIONS:

1. Share and discuss poem from Activity 8.12, Homework.
2. Think about significant memories in your life.
3. Describe these memories in words or pictures and compare them to the present as shown in these examples.

EXAMPLES:

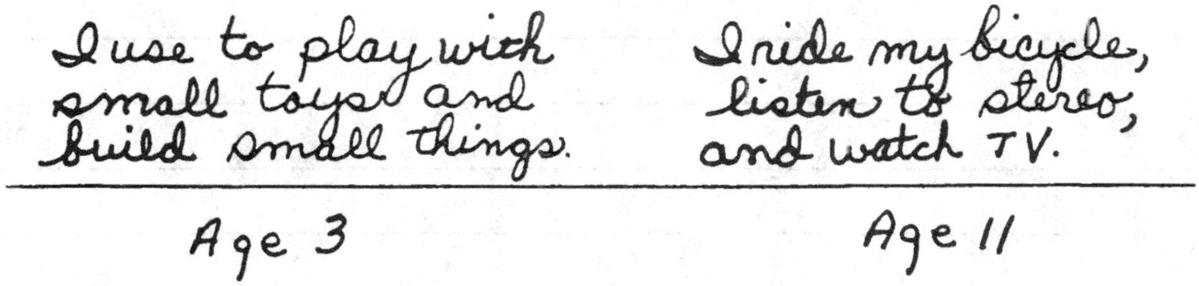

4. Share your memories and your pictures with others in the group and discuss how the changes took place.

5. Write some summary statements about how you have changed and then share with the group.

   Examples: I have changed in size with the passage of time. I now have more responsibilities than I had when I was younger.

HOMEWORK:

Write a situation about which you are going to be making a decision soon.

Name ______________________________

Date ______________ Hour ______________

Activity 8.14
PUTTING DECISION MAKING INTO ACTION

GOAL:

To practice making effective decisions with others.

DIRECTIONS:

1. Bring to class a decision you are trying to make. (This is the Homework from Activity 8.13).

2. Divide into groups of three people in each group.

3. Role-play helping each other with decision making. Use those skills you have learned including:

   Five-Step Problem Solving (Activity 8.8)

   Caring—Listening With Your Body (Module 3)

   Empathy (Module 4)

   Paraphrasing (Activities 4.2 and 4.3)

   Brainstorming (Activity 8.11)

   Using "I" Messsages (Module 5)

   Values Identification (Module 8)

   Goal Setting (Module 8)

   In the role-playing, one of you will play the helper, one will play the helpee using the situation that person wrote in the Homework for Activity 8.13, and one person will be the observer. The observer will give feedback after the helpee and helper have finished.

____

____

____

____

____

In the role-playing proceed through the "Five-steps in Decision Making" and use your other skills as well. A step-by-step procedure for helping others in decision making might be outlined as follows:

Five-Steps in Decision Making **Have Helpee Do**	**Peer Helping Skills** **Helper Does**
1. State problem clearly.	Caring: Listen With Your Body Empathy
2. Search for alternatives.	Encourages brainstorming
3. List pros and cons for each alternative. (Identifies Consequences)	"I" Messages Values Identification Paraphrasing Decision Making
4. Choose the best alternative	Goal Setting
5. Check it out with a trusted adult.	Empathy Caring: Listening With Your Body Paraphrasing

Observer can use the preceding outline to check what the helpee and helper do and to what extent. This can be the basis for giving helpful feedback to both—helpee and helper.

4. After the observer has given feedback, switch roles and repeat Item 3.

5. Repeat Item 4 so that all have had a chance to play all three roles.

6. Discuss as a group what occurred, how you can be of assistance to others, additional things on which you need to practice, and some of your own values that might need to be explored more so as to be of greater assistance to others.

Name ______________________

Date ____________ Hour ____________

Activity 8.15
GOAL SETTING

GOAL:

To learn to set achievable goals.

DIRECTIONS:

1. Listen as your leader explains the importance of setting clear goals.

2. Think about the things you love to do the most in life like going out to eat, bike riding, swimming, playing basketball or baseball, traveling, etc. As fast as you can list ten to twenty things you love to do.

$	M-F	W-X-Y		THINGS I LOVE TO DO
____	________	____________	a.	______________________
____	________	____________	b.	______________________
____	________	____________	c.	______________________
____	________	____________	d.	______________________
____	________	____________	e.	______________________
____	________	____________	f.	______________________
____	________	____________	g.	______________________
____	________	____________	h.	______________________
____	________	____________	i.	______________________
____	________	____________	j.	______________________
____	________	____________	k.	______________________
____	________	____________	l.	______________________
____	________	____________	m.	______________________
____	________	____________	n.	______________________
____	________	____________	o.	______________________
____	________	____________	p.	______________________
____	________	____________	q.	______________________
____	________	____________	r.	______________________
____	________	____________	w.	______________________
____	________	____________	t.	______________________

3. Do the following:

   a. Place a "$" sign opposite each thing you love to do that costs over $10.00 each time you do it.

   b. Place a "M" if your mother would do it, a "F" if your father would do it, and "M-F" if both would do it.

   c. Place a "W" if you did it this past week, "X" if you did it during the past two to six weeks, and "Y" if you did it this past year.

4. Review your list and summarize some statements about things you love to do. Write these summary statements.

   Examples:

   The things I like to do are generally inexpensive.

   The things I like to do are things I can do with my parents.

   ____

   ____

   ____

   ____

   ____

   ____

5. Turn to the "Goal Setting" sheet. Now think about something you love to do and write a goal to do it.

   Example:

   I will wash my hands each time before I eat.

   Use the guidelines to see if this is a good goal:

   Achievable—Yes, I always eat at home or in restaurants and a wash room is near.

   Measurable—Yes, because I can keep record as to whether I do or do not wash.

   Desirable—Yes, because this will help keep me healthy.

   Stated positively—Yes, because it states what I will do.

   Helpful—Yes, because it establishes specifics of what and when I am to act.

Name ______________________

Date ____________ Hour ____________

My goal is ______________________

____

____

____

Achieveable— ______________________

____

____

____

Measurable— ______________________

____

____

____

Desirable— ______________________

____

____

____

Helpful— ______________________

____

____

____

GOAL SETTING

Success in daily living can be enhanced by action-talking about "what I want to do" and actually doing it are different. The use of goal setting is a means to action. The following guidelines will help make goals successful:

1. Goals must be ACHIEVABLE.
2. Goals must be MEASURABLE.
3. Goals must be DESIRABLE.
4. Goals must be stated POSITIVELY.
5. Goals must be HELPFUL.

Here is a goal I will set for myself:

I will____________________________________

____

by__________________________________(date)

____

Signature

MODULE 9
PUTTING PEER-HELPING SKILLS INTO ACTION

PUTTING PEER HELPING SKILLS INTO ACTION

As you begin to put your skills into action through different projects, you might want to go back to Module 2, Activity 2.4, "Self Inventory of Helping Skills" to learn how you have grown in terms of your skills.

Before starting on your projects, it is important that your leader has spent time explaining the project and training you in specifics of the project. An example might be if you are a tutor, you will need to learn specific tutoring skills after you have learned the basic skills.

Next, as you work on the projects, it is important that your leader continue to supervise you and give you support and help you deal with any problems that may arise.

As you begin to work in the peer-helping field, people begin to respond to you differently. Therefore, it is important to know how to practice peer helping in responsible ways. These activities will help you understand the process of knowing your limits.

Name ______________________________

Date ______________ Hour ______________

Activity 9.1
THINGS TO THINK ABOUT

GOAL:

To understand the importance of training.

DIRECTIONS:

1. Look at the following list of things to think about in training as well as during your projects and add to this list, if appropriate.

   a. Confidentiality

      (1) The person you are trying to help must trust you.

      (2) Things learned as a helper must only be shared with the leader.

   b. Participation

      (1) Attend training classes.

      (2) Become involved by role-playing and discussion.

      (3) Practice the skills taught appropriately.

   c. Time to Practice

      (1) Allow time to do homework.

      (2) Spend time with your leader getting feedback during the project.

   d. Supervision

      (1) Expect supervision during activity.

      (2) Help the supervisor to know when supervision would be most helpful with each situation in which you are a peer helper.

      (3) Discuss with the supervisor after and in some cases during supervision.

2. Work in small groups to discuss any additional issues and then share them with the class.

3. Read and share ideas related to "Code of Ethics for Peer Helpers" produced by National Peer Helpers Association.

NATIONAL PEER HELPERS ASSOCIATION
CODE OF ETHICS*
FOR PEER HELPERS

Peer Helpers shall be people of personal integrity. As a minimum, the NPHA believes the peer helpers Code of Ethics shall contain the following and be evidenced by a commitment to and pursuit of:

1. A philosophy which upholds peer helping as an effective way to address the needs and conditions of people.

2. The individual's right to dignity, self-development, and self-direction.

3. Supervision and support from professional staff while involved in the program.

4. The development of a nuturing personality which:

    - Reflects a positive role model and healthy lifestyle (i.e., development and observation of a set of norms which guide behavior while in the program).

    - Rejects the pursuit of personal power, elitist status, or gain at the expense of others.

    - Strives to exemplify the peer helping philosophy in all life situations.

5. Maintenance of confidentiality of information imparted during the course of program-related activities. While confidentiality is the norm, certain exceptions shall be referred immediately to the professional staff. These exceptions include the following:

    - Situations involving real or potential danger to the safety or well-being of the peer helper, helpee, or others.

    - Child abuse, sexual abuse, and other situations involving legal requirements of disclosure.

    - Severe family dysfunction, psychotic behavior, extreme drug or alcohol abuse, and any other problems beyond the experience and expertise of the peer helper.

6. Personal Safety

    Peer helpers must recognize, report, and know techniques to deal with potential threats to their emotional or physical well-being.

---

* A Code of Ethics is an agreement among those who commit to the program as to the norms which shall guide their behaior during their involvement in the program.

Name ______________________

Date ____________ Hour ____________

Activity 9.2
GUIDELINES

GOAL:

To develop individual guidelines as you work in your school setting as a peer helper.

INTRODUCTION:

To operate within your school as a peer helper certain guidelines and procedures must be followed in order for you to be in the role of the peer helper.

The following are general areas that you need to develop specific to your school. Write them as your leader discusses rules.

DIRECTIONS:

1. Write "Peer Helping School Rules" that you must follow.

____

____

____

____

____

____

2. Write "Peer Helping Requirements" that I must do in order to be active as a peer helper.

____

____

____

____

____

____

3. Write "Specific Guidlines" for peer helpers in each of the following areas:

   a. Confidentiality ____

   ____

   ____

   b. Participation ____

   ____

   ____

   c. Supervision ____

   ____

   ____

   d. Adequate Training ____

   ____

   ____

   e. Project Guidelines ____

   ____

   ____

   f. Others (specify) ____

   ____

   ____

4. Sign this sheet as your willingness to be a peer helper, to follow the rules and guidelines, and to cooperate with your leader.

> I am aware of the preceding rules and guidelines for my school and my Peer Helping Program and agree to follow them. I also agree to adhere to NPHA "Ethics for Peer Helpers."
>
> Students signature ________________________ Date: ________

5. Meet with your leader and discuss these rules and guidelines and have the leader to sign verifying that you two have talked and are willing to work together as a peer helper.

Leader's Signature ________________________________ Date ________

Name ______________________________

Date ______________ Hour ______________

Activity 9.3
PEER HELPER'S GUIDE FOR KNOWING LIMITS

GOAL:

To assist you in knowing your limits as a peer helper.

INTRODUCTION

You need to realize that you are a helper and not a counselor. Your role is to provide assistance to another peer in projects and activities on which you and your teacher decide. To insure that you do stay within the limit of your training, you will need to have regular contact with your peer helper leader as you are involved in delivering your project.

DIRECTIONS:

1. Review with your leader and write the meaning of the following two words as they are used in peer helping program:

   a. Confidentiality ______________________________

   ____

   b. Supervision ______________________________

   ____

2. Discuss limits of peer helping—specific situations in which you are to make a referral and/or discuss immediately the situation with your leader. These include the following:

   a. Student considering suicide.
   b. Student abusing alcohol or drugs.
   c. Student that has been abused by an adult.
   d. Serious emotional or learning problems.
   e. Others (specify). ______________________________

   ____

3. Discuss as a group and with your leader the referral sources and guidelines for the local community, school, or group in which you are a peer helper. Write these for your reference as the leader approves each.

Source and/or Person	**Mechanisms (Guidelines)** **Ways to refer to or make use of** **the source and/or person**
Example: peer helper leader	a. Talk with leader about the situation b. Take the person to the leader if the situation necessitates immediate action.

4. Discuss with your leader and the group what is meant by conflict of interest and write illustrations of where or when this might occur and as a result you would not be the one to be the peer helper to the person.

Example:

Best friend tutoring.

Others (specify) ______________________________

5. Work in small groups and discuss the following four situations. List what you would do and why.

HOW WOULD YOU HANDLE . . . ?

a. During the time you are tutoring another student in math, she discusses the fact that she is down and has considered taking some pills she found in the medicine cabinet. What would you do?

____

____

b. During the time you are showing a new student around school, you learn that an adult hit the student and there are marks on his or her body. What would you do?

____

____

c. As you are organizing a game on the playground with a group of students that appear to be loners, one of them shares with you that they have been using pot for the last three months. What would you do?

____

____

d. As you talk with another student that has a handicap, she discusses some serious family problem that seems overwhelming. What would you do?

____

____

6. Discuss as a total group, responses from the small groups to the four situations in Item 5.

7. Review your understanding of

a. Why referral is essential with many people, ______________________________

____

b. When to make referrals (what kinds of situations are not for you as a peer helper), and ______________________________

____

c. Sources and/or people to whom you can make a referral of the person or go to talk about the situation. ______________________________

____

Name ______________________________

Date ______________ Hour ______________

Activity 9.4
WHAT CAN I DO?

GOAL:

To understand the goals of my role as a peer helper.

DIRECTIONS:

1. Make a list of activities and projects that you feel you are presently qualified to do.

   Examples:

   a. Be a friend to a new student.

   b. Tutor others in spelling.

   c. Talk daily with another student who has no friends or a limited number of friends.

   d. Invite a lonely student to play at recess.

WHAT I CAN DO

DIRECTIONS: List specific activities and projects that you feel you are presently qualified to do.

____

____

____

____

____

____

____

____

____

____

2. Have your leader initial each of the ones in your list that the leader agrees that you are qualified to do at this time.

3. Role-play some situations in which you will make a referral. You might make up your own situations or use one of the four in Activity 9.2, Item 5.

4. Make a list of things you would like to do but need additional training.

   Example: Lead a small group discussion.

THINGS I WOULD LIKE TO DO BUT NEED ADDITIONAL TRAINING

DIRECTIONS: List these one-by-one and be as specific as you can.

____

____

____

____

____

____

____

____

____

5. Sign and date this activity.

   I agree to help my peers in the areas that my leader and I feel I have the skills to perform.

   Name ______________________________ Date ____________

PART II

APPLICATION OF SKILLS

Supplementary Activities

INTRODUCTION

The skills you have previously learned are the foundation of your Peer Helping roles. These roles will vary from situation to situation and will vary depending on your skills.

The supplementary activities in Part II of this book will help you perform your peer helping assignment more effectively.

Listen to your leader give you directions on how to do your peer helping activities. You will need to meet with your leader on a regular basis to review skills learned previously and to learn new skills explained in the supplementary activities.

I'm A Winner!
I have surroundings all my own.
I have my own look.
I have many different feelings.
I have many talents.
I have people who care.
I have some things to work on.
We're All O.K.!
Everyone's Unique!
We're All Special!
It's Great Being Me!

Name ______________________________

Date ____________ Hour ____________

Application of Skills No. 1
MAKING INITIAL CONTACT WITH ANOTHER

GOAL:

To help give you some ways to approach comfortably other students in school.

DIRECTIONS:

1. Think about a time when you were new to a group. First write what you remember about this experience and how you felt.

____

____

____

____

____

____

____

2. Share these experiences and feelings from Direction No. 1 with your group.
3. Think about anyone that helped you feel more comfortable in this new experience. Write the behaviors of this person or persons that helped you in this new situation. What did the person do that helped?

____

____

____

____

4. Share these behaviors for question 3 with your group.

5. Compile a list of helpful behaviors that you could use to approach students who might be new or lonely.

____

____

____

____

____

____

6. Write a situation on a card that would involve a student being new to a group. Have all group members place all cards in a box and spend some time drawing a card at a time out of the box. Have two people role-playing the situation with one person new to the group and the other person being the peer helper. After each role-play, discuss with your leader the behaviors that helped the new person feel welcome. Make a summary list of helpful behaviors that can be done by the peer helper.

____

____

____

____

____

____

HOMEWORK:

Within the next few days identify someone in school whom you think is lonely or new. Apply your peer helper behaviors to make the person feel more a part of the group. Record what happened and at the next peer helper session discuss with the group:

1. how you approached the person,

2. how the conversation proceeded,

3. how the person responded to you,

4. how you felt, and

5. what you gained from the experience.

Name ______________________________

Date ______________ Hour ______________

Application of Skills No. 2
COMPLIMENTARY YOURS

GOAL:

To help you learn to give compliments to others in order for positive relationships to occur.

DIRECTIONS:

1. Think about compliments and answers to the following:

   a. How often do you give others compliments? ______________________________

   ____

   b. What kind of compliments do you give? ______________________________

   ____

   c. What kind do you like to receive? ______________________________

   ____

   d. What feelings come when you receive a compliment? ______________________________

   ____

2. Put your name on the page of hearts. Pass it around the group, and put a compliment on one of the hearts on each person's sheet. When you get yours back, read your hearts. Decide which compliment felt the best and discuss with your group. How does it feel to receive a whole list of compliments?

   ____

   ____

3. Decide to give one compliment a day making sure you include the shy or lonely student that you want to feel welcome. Record the compliment you gave and the reaction of the person. Be ready to share this experience during the next class.

   a. Compliment ______________________________

   ____

   b. Reaction ______________________________

   ____

Name:________________________________

Write a compliment to the person whose name is at the top of the page.

Name ______________________________

Date ______________ Hour ______________

Application of Skills No. 3
FRIENDS FOREVER

GOAL:

To understand how I relate better to others.

DIRECTIONS:

1. Think about and write an answer to these questions:

a. Why do we need people?

____

____

____

b. What would it be like if we were alone?

____

____

____

2. Look at the word "relationships." Write the different types of relationships you have.

____

____

____

3. Identify and write ways your relationships have changed over the years and then discuss these with other peer helper members.

____

____

____

4. Do the "Privacy Squares Worksheet" in class. This is a technique that you also can do when you work with your peer support group. But first, do it with your peer helpers to practice. Do the activity and then choose a few situations to discuss.

5. After completing "Privacy Squares Worksheet" complete these sentences:

   a. I notice that I ____

   ____

   b. I learned that I ____

   ____

6. Break into small groups to discuss your privacy squares. Use the following four questions as guidelines for discussion.

   a. What kinds of things did you place in the inner square?

   b. What kinds of things did you place in the outer square?

   c. To whom were you willing to tell the most things?

   d. Would you like to change your privacy square?

HOMEWORK:

Do this activity with your peer support group either with an individual or with a group. Be sure to discuss these things:

1. As human beings, we have many needs. We could call these inner and outer or physical and emotional needs. Be sure to discuss with your students the importance of getting both needs met. That is why we must all learn to be supportive and helpful to one another.

2. Assign students in your group the task of showing emotional support to someone in his or her life and to record what happened.

Name ______________________________

Date ______________ Hour ______________

PRIVACY SQUARES WORKSHEET

We have many types of relationships. Some are close and some are very casual. We are going to look closer at these relationships.

1. Some things in our lives we would be glad to let anyone know—favorite color, TV show, or movie star. We put these relationships in the category of ***strangers,*** because we don't know these people very well.

2. Some things we might not want strangers to know, however we would be willing to tell ***acquaintances,*** people we know casually.

3. Still other things we reserve only for our ***friends.***

4. Some thoughts and feelings we would only be willing to share with our ***best friends.***

5. Some things we would only be willing to share with our ***family.***

6. Finally, some things we might not want to share with anyone but ***ourselves.***

On the next page are squares with these previously listed six classifications of people. Think about these six classifications of people and decide which ones you would be willing to share information and what kind, if any.

To assist you in the process ten situations are listed. For each situation place the key word in the square with the person with whom you would be willing to share that information. The key word is in quote marks.

Who would you be willing to tell. . .(Write key word only).

1. That you were really "***good***" at something?
2. That you had a personal "***health***" problem?
3. When you "***cried***" the last time?
4. What "***grade***" you are in?
5. What your favorite "***TV***" show is?
6. What you "***dislike***" about your friends?
7. That you had a "***nightmare?***"
8. That you had a "***crush***" on someone in your class?
9. What your favorite "***meal***" is?
10. That you "***cheated***" on a test?

PRIVACY SQUARES

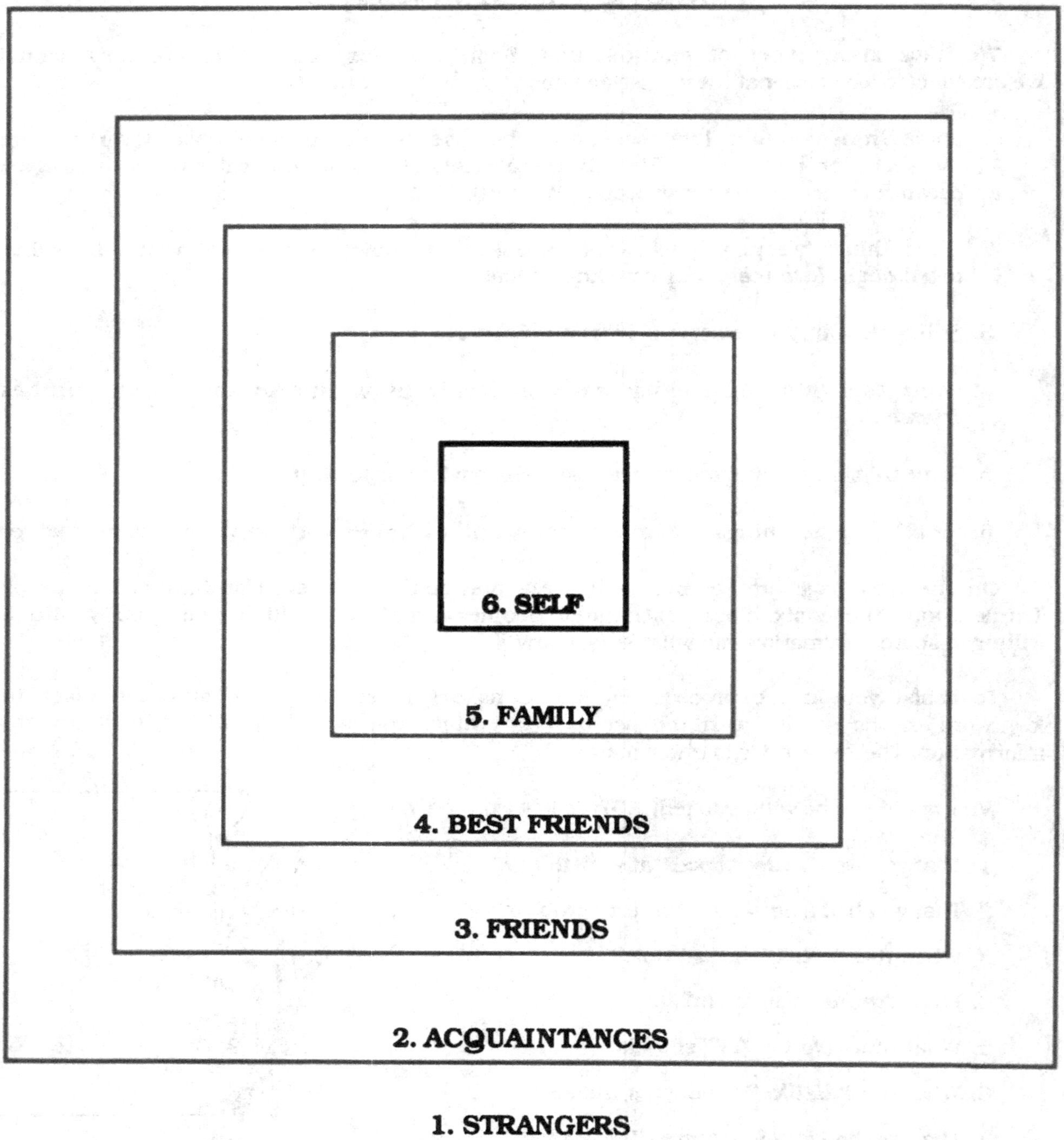

Name ______________________

Date ____________ Hour ____________

Application of Skills No. 4
POT OF GOLD

GOAL:

To help you learn some ways to help yourself and others set some important goals.

DIRECTIONS:

1. Read the "Pot of Gold" activity sheet. Five goals are listed on the sheet and assigned to pots of gold. Color the goal you would set for yourself.

2. Think about steps that you might take to help get you to your pot of gold. Write those steps on your "Pot of Gold" worksheet.

3. Think about how you might use this sheet in your work with the tutoring program. Could you use this sheet in helping others set goals?

____

____

____

____

HOMEWORK:

1. Take a blank worksheet and use this "Pot of Gold" activity in your next session. Help the student set his or her own goal.

2. Write your experience.

____

____

____

____

____

POT OF GOLD

Which Pot of Gold would you most like to find at the end of your rainbow? Color that pot gold.

EXAMPLES:

1. Make good grades.

2. Become a star in sports.

3. Have enough money so my family and I can do what we want to do.

4. Solve the problem of world peace.

5. Be poplar.

6. Other (List) ______________________________

____

Make up a plan that will help you reach your pot of gold. Write the first three steps that you will take in order to get to the end of the rainbow.

1. ______________________________

____

2. ______________________________

____

3. ______________________________

____

Name ____________________

Date ____________ Hour ____________

Application of Skills No. 5
IMPROVING STUDY SKILLS

GOAL:

To help you learn a simple study skill that you can teach others.

DIRECTIONS:

1. Read over the "SQ3R Study Skill" sheet in your workbook.

2. Discuss the five steps with your leader.

3. Practice teaching this technique to a partner in your peer helper training class.

4. Write how this method could be used to help you learn better the material in school.

____

____

____

____

5. Identify how you might use this material with the students you are tutoring.

____

____

____

____

HOMEWORK:

1. Use this technique for your next reading assignment in class.

2. Record how this process helped you.

____

____

____

3. Use this technique in a tutoring session. Write about the experience and discuss in class how successful it was.

SQ3R STUDY SKILL

S—Survey . . . Quickly look over the chapter title, section headings, and chapter summary to get an idea of what the chapter is about. You are skimming the material to get a general idea of what the chapter is telling you.

Q—Question . . . Go back to the beginning of the chapter; turn the first heading into a question so you know what you're trying to find out when you're reading.

R—Read . . . Read that section to find the answer to your question.

R—Recite . . . Tell yourself the answer by taking brief notes for that section. Write the question on the left side of your paper, the notes on the right. Repeat the question, Read and Recite steps for each section of your assignment. Do each step over until you thoroughly understand what you have read.

R—Review . . . Cover the right side of your paper; ask yourself the questions on the left and answer them. If you can't answer the questions, go over your notes.

Name ______________________________

Date ______________ Hour ______________

Application of Skills No. 6
HOW TO LISTEN IN CLASS

GOAL:

To help you understand the importance of listening in order to learn.

DIRECTIONS:

1. When you are helping others learn, understand that helping them listen will really help them improve their learning. Most students who do poorly in school only "half listen" to what the teacher says. When it comes time to do homework or get ready for a test, these students have trouble because they have inadequate material. Read the rewards of listening on your "How to Listen in Class" study sheet. Check the ones that mean the most to you.

2. Listen to your leader and classmates—other peer helpers. Remind yourself about how you show you are listening. (Caring: Listen with your body skill, Module 3, is an excellent summary.) Sit up and forward, ***clear your mind,*** and really tune in to the person who is talking, supplying significant information.

3. Make a list of benefits from listening that might be possible for you.

   What happens as you listen carefully? Do you remember more of what the speaker says? What else do you notice when you listen?

   ____

   ____

HOMEWORK:

1. For the next day, really focus on listening. Try to listen with all your might during a class. Practice listening to your teacher. Look at the teacher. Raise your hand and show interest. Record what happens.

   ____

   ____

   ____

2. Complete the "How to Listen in Class Worksheet" and answer the five important facts you learned because you listened.

HOW TO LISTEN IN CLASS

If you really listen, you will earn rewards.

You might:

—find that a subject you thought dull is really interesting

—find that the work becomes easier

—learn more about the personalities of your teacher and classmates

—discover leads to answering questions in other subjects

—be surprised that class time goes by so quickly

By listening, you can learn, not only from the teacher, but also from your classmates when they are giving reports, or taking part in a general discussion.

Write five important facts you learned today because you listened:

1. ______________________________

____

____

2. ______________________________

____

____

3. ______________________________

____

____

4. ______________________________

____

____

5. ______________________________

____

____

Name ______________________________

Date ______________ Hour ______________

Application of Skills No. 7
STUDY IDEAS

GOAL:

To give you more ideas about how to help others and yourself study better.

DIRECTIONS:

1. Look over the "Study Ideas" worksheet. Discuss these in your peer helper training session and make sure each idea is understood.

2. Use the "Study Ideas" worksheet with one of the students in the peer tutoring program.

3. Use the following explanation to introduce the worksheet and the idea of a study habit. Explain that a study habit is a routine that is followed regularly. Talk about the following benefits that come about from using proper study habits:

   a. improvement in the type of work turned in,

   b. more enjoyment from school work,

   c. pleasure in learning more difficult work, and

   d. fewer worries as the student gets better.

4. Tell the student with whom you are working that repeating material is a really important way to learn. Tell the student that often pacing back and forth and talking out loud also are ways to learn from students who learn best from ***HEARING*** material. Tell students that most people learn from the following ways:

   a. through seeing something—by demonstrations or audio-visual aids;

   b. through hearing—by listening to a tape or a teacher;

   c. through motion—by moving our bodies in some way; and

   d. through touch—by feeling differences in consistency, weight, and texture.

5. Use the "Study Ideas" worksheet with students you are working with, and have them practice in class. Have them write how using this technique helped them. You might ask them to keep a notebook.

STUDY IDEAS!

1 Listen carefully.

2. Take notes.

3. Ask questions.

4. Watch visual aids.

5. Read the notes each night.

6. List questions for the teacher.

7. Study for a test four days before.

8. Try studying out loud.

9. Get a good night's sleep before a test.

10. Read notes carefully before the day of the test.

11. Eat a well-balanced meal before a test.

Name ____________________

Date __________ Hour __________

Application of Skills No. 8
BEHAVIORAL CONTRACT

GOAL:

To help you commit to learning certain things, and changing your behavior in positive ways by signing a contract.

INTRODUCTION

You can use a behavioral contract both for yourself in a variety of peer helping programs, and also for the students with whom you work.

DIRECTIONS:

1. Discuss with your leader what learnings you will need for the particular type of student and program that you will be working with. For examples of how to write these, see "Behavioral Contract Examples" 1 and 2 and read Items 1a and 1b in both.

2. Discuss the skills you will need to work with the type of program in which you are involved. Think about this and have your leader help you decide specific skills that you will need to master. For examples of how to write these see "Behavioral Contract Examples" 1 and 2 and read Items 2a and 2b in both.

3. Think about how you will be able to determine whether or not you are having success. These need to be stated in specific ways to determine. For examples of how to write these see "Behavioral Contract Examples: 1 and 2 and read Items 3a and 3b in both.

4. Identify a specific peer helper role that you might have. Then complete the "Behavioral Contract" by writing (a) what you will need to learn, (b) what skills you will use, and how you will determine success.

5. Discuss with your group how it feels to write these very specific learnings.

6. Talk about what writing these down does for your commitment to the goals you have set.

HOMEWORK:

1. Use the behavioral contract with one of the students with whom you are working.

2. Record what happens when ***YOU*** do this with another person. Is it difficult to get someone else to do a contract? What did you learn about how to help others commit to goals?

BEHAVIORAL CONTRACT EXAMPLES

Example 1: Contract for Peer Helper in elementary school aid program. For my peer helping class, I promise to do these things:

1. To learn

   a. how to help others set goals, and

   b. how to help others learn to study better.

2. To help others I will learn well skills in

   a. goal setting (as shown in Module 8), and

   b. studying (as shown in application of skills AOS 5, AOS 6, and AOS 7).

3. Evidence of my success will be

   a. when I can get the student I am helping to write a specific goal, and

   b. when I can get the student I am helping to express positive feelings about his or her studying behavior.

Signed ____ (Peer Helper)

Signed ____ (Leader)

Name ______________________________

Date ______________ Hour ______________

Example 2: Contract for Peer Helper helping a student with personal problems.

1. To learn

   a. how to help the person express his or her problems.

   b. how to help the person state correctly his or her problems.

2. To help others I will learn well skills in

   a. listening (as shown in Module 3).

   b. empathy (as shown in Module 4).

3. Evidence of my success will be

   a. when I can get the student to state his or her problem very specifically without all the if, when, only, etc.

   b. when I can gain his or her confidence well enough that the total problem is shared with me.

Signed ____ (Peer Helper)

Signed ____ (Leader)

BEHAVIORAL CONTRACT

For my peer helping class, I promise to do these things:

1. To learn ______________________________

____

____

____

2. To help others I will learn well skills in ______________________________

____

____

____

3. Evidence of my success will be ______________________________

____

____

____

Signed: ______________________________ (Helper)

Signed: ______________________________ (Leader)

Name ______________________

Date ____________ Hour ____________

Application of Skills No. 9
ROLE-PLAYING

GOAL:

To help you learn to use role-playing in helping other students to resist peer group pressure.

DIRECTIONS:

1. Read over the "Role-Play Worksheet" having to do with "learning to say no" to peer group pressure.

2. Discuss how to role-play with your leader and members of your peer helper learning group. Volunteers will act out the scene, and the rest of the class will "process" the role-play and talk about the skill involved. Class members will help each other with the skill until it gets better and better.

3. Decide if this is a skill that you want to learn, and consider adding it to your behavioral contract. Begin practicing this skill daily, or whenever the opportunity comes, and record what happens.

____

____

____

____

____

ROLE-PLAY WORKSHEET

PURPOSE OF ROLE-PLAY:

The reason we role-play is to practice a new skill in front of people who can help us improve the skill.

PROCEDURE FOR ROLE-PLAY:

1. Think about a situation where you would have trouble saying "no" to friends who want you to do something you shouldn't do. Write that situation here.

____

____

____

____

____

2. Ask members of the group to act out the scene with someone practicing some friendly, but firm ways to say "no."

3. Discuss with your group any ways that the person could improve with the ways they said "no."

4. Share your feelings about what happened. Record below any new skill on which you need to work.

____

____

____

____

____

Name ____________________

Date ____________ Hour ____________

Application of Skills No. 10
DIFFERENT STROKES FOR DIFFERENT FOLKS

GOAL:

To learn that differences among people are normal.

DIRECTIONS:

1. Think about the idea that differences among people are okay. Some differences are easier to accept than others. Look at the list below and evaluate how each statement applies to you.

	Strongly Agree	Agree		Disagee	Strongly Disagree
	5	4	3	2	1
a. Baseball is my favorite sport.	____	____	____	____	____
b. I like to try new kinds of foods.	____	____	____	____	____
c. After school, I like to be by myself for awhile.	____	____	____	____	____
d. I like to have a lot of friends.	____	____	____	____	____
e. Being successful in school is the most important thing to me.	____	____	____	____	____

2. Share your evaluations with others in your peer helper training group and have them share with you. Discuss the differences and among persons in your group and why the differences.

3. Write how you felt when you were different from most of the other students.

____

____

____

____

4. Write about the extent to which you believe your group members were able to accept differences among people.

5. Review your thoughts about what kind of differences are problems for some people and what you think might be done about them? Write those thoughts in the space provided.

Kinds of Differences That Are Problems for Some People	Thoughts About What Might Be Done to Help

Name ______________________________

Date ______________ Hour ______________

Application of Skills No. 11
THE REAL UNDERDOG

GOAL:

To help you understand how students act when they are insecure and do not like themselves. This will help you understand why these students do and say certain things, and can help you learn ways of dealing with this type of student.

DIRECTIONS:

1. Read the handout titled "The Real Underdog." Discuss with your peer helper training group some of the ways you have noticed that these students act when they do not like themselves.

2. Complete the bottom part of "The Real Underdog" sheet.

3. Summarize in your words the major differences between people with good self images and those with poor self image.

4. Write some behaviors that you have had

   a. when you felt good ______________________________

   ____

   b. when you felt bad ______________________________

   ____

5. Summarize what you believe about how people feel whenever you are being a peer helper with them.

6. Write how you believe such understanding will help you when you try to help others.

____

____

____

HOMEWORK:

1. Notice someone's behavior who seems not to like himself or herself.

2. Record these behaviors in the space provided.

"THE REAL UNDERDOG"

Listed below are different ways students act. Students do some of these things because they actually do not like themselves. They are not happy with themselves. But, they do not want anyone to know this, so they will do some of the things in the list below. Students who like themselves, feel good about themselves, and are happy and fun to be around also will do some of the things in the list below.

1. Shows off
2. Is loud and noisy
3. Acts cool
4. Laughs a lot
5. Always has to be the boss
6. Laughs at people
7. Takes turns
8. Cons people
9. Lies
10. Picks on people
11. Always has to pick for teams
12. Makes fun of others
13. Is polite and courteous
14. Usually is agreeable
15. Says funny things
16. Is proud of self
17. Helps others
18. Listens to others
19. Is at ease with people
20. Takes advice

Directions:

1. Write the things in the first column you think the people do who like themselves. And, write the things in the second column you think the people do who do not like themselves.

Good Self Image	**Poor Self Image**
1. ______________	1. ______________
2. ______________	2. ______________
3. ______________	3. ______________
4. ______________	4. ______________
5. ______________	5. ______________
6. ______________	6. ______________
7. ______________	7. ______________
8. ______________	8. ______________
9. ______________	9. ______________
10. ______________	10. ______________

2. Discuss your choices with other peer helpers and see if they made the same choices. If not, discuss the reasons for each other's choices.

Name ____________________________

Date ______________ Hour ______________

Application of Skills No. 12
PEER PRESSURE SITUATIONS

GOAL:

This will help you understand peer pressure, and how it affects the way people behave.

DIRECTIONS:

1. Discuss the following situations that show peer pressure.

   a. You are in a class where you wanted to raise your hand to ask a question of a guest speaker, but you looked around and nobody else had a hand raised, so you didn't raise your hand.

   b. The teacher asked a question and when you looked around the room, everybody had a hand raised except you. You raised your hand too.

2. Share some experiences about when you have felt this kind of pressure. How did it feel?

   ____

   ____

   ____

3. Use the "Role-Playing Activities" sheet and act some of these out where peer pressure is involved.

4. Discuss your feelings after each situation.

5. Decide which situations create the most pressure.

HOMEWORK:

1. Notice this week any time you experience pressure from anyone. Record how you responded to the pressure.

   ____

   ____

   ____

2. On what do you need to work to help you resist peer pressure?

   ____

   ____

   ____

ROLE-PLAYING ACTIVITIES

Problem Situations for One Main Character

In the following situations, one child can take the primary responsibility for the talking and action; the other person(s) can serve as "props."

1. A shy schoolmate has returned after a sickness of several weeks. You want to make him feel at home in school again.

2. You see one child teasing another.

3. A classmate jumps on you, or hits you in trying to say, "hello."

4. You and a classmate are walking through a department store. He tries to get you to steal something.

5. You're walking home from school, and see a boy who is a bully. He hits children or snatches their books.

6. Another student has just torn up the homework you spent all last evening doing.

7. A child grabs the ball during a game and starts to run away.

8. A friend takes you aside and tells you a secret so that the other friend that you are with can't hear.

9. You see a teacher with her arms full of books. She needs the door opened. You open the door and ask if you can help her. At that moment a child calls out, "Teacher's pet!"

10. A classmate says, "Can't you do better than that?" while you are both drawing pictures. You know that he is really unhappy, and you want to help him.

11. Your friends tease you whenever you volunteer in class. What do you do or say?

Name ______________________

Date ______________ Hour ______________

Application of Skills No. 13
PEER PRESSURE WITH DRUGS AND ALCOHOL

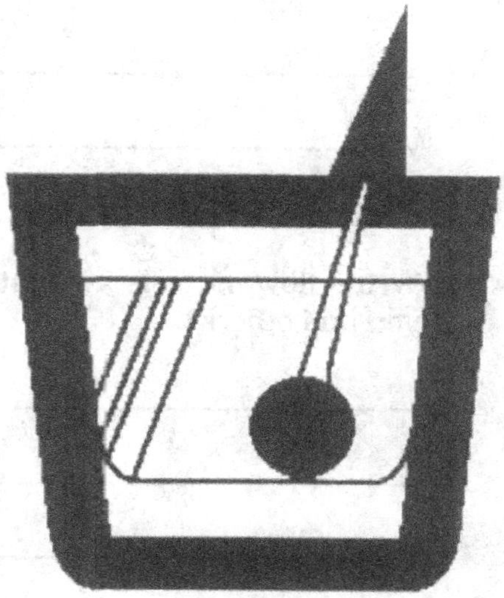

GOAL:

To help you obtain some ideas to help you resist peer pressure with drugs and alcohol.

DIRECTIONS:

1. Examine the "Peer Pressure Tactics" list. Discuss this with your class and list any techniques and tactics that could be used to avoid peer pressure to use drugs.

2. Write a role-play that you might have seen or heard about regarding peer pressure with drugs and alcohol. Role-play it with the group, and find a good solution to that kind of pressure.

____

____

____

____

3. Identify kinds of pressure that peers often use.

____

____

____

____

4. Identify kinds of positive things you might use when you want to resist pressure?

____

____

____

____

HOMEWORK:

1. Write about a situation where someone resists peer pressure really well. Record this.

____

____

____

2. Write how it feels to resist peer pressure. How will resisting peer pressure help you and others?

____

____

____

3. What techniques will you use to help others resist peer pressure?

____

____

____

PEER PRESSURE TACTICS

1. THINK STRONG
2. Stay Calm
3. Say "No"
4. Ask A Question
5. Send an "I" Message
6. Come Up With a Good Idea
7. Shift Groups
8. Go to Another
9. Move to Safety
10. Seek Adult Help

NOTES

NOTES

NOTES

NOTES

ABOUT THE AUTHORS

JUDITH TINDALL, Ph.D., has been a psychologist, counselor, and consultant since 1965. She is presently a psychologist with Rohen and Associates Psychological Center and a Consultant for Industri-Care, a division of Rohen and Associates in St. Charles, Missouri. She is Co-Director of the W.E.L. Eating Disorder Program. She was also Associate Professor at University of Missouri at St. Louis and has taught graduate courses for Webster University. She has worked 18 years in public schools as a counselor and guidance director.

She has held local, state, and national offices in professional associations, such as, St. Louis Association of Counseling and Development, Missouri Association of Counseling and Development, American Association of Counseling and Development, and American School Counselors Association. She was responsible for the development of American School Counselors Association First Leadership Conference.

She has received outstanding Professional Service Awards from both St. Louis A.C.D. and Missouri A.C.D. She also co-authored and successfully led the effort to pass state legislation benefiting counselors. She currently serves on the Missouri Committee of Professional Counselors. She is on the Board of Directors for the National Peer Helpers Association in which she was the co-director of the first national conference and chairperson of the Standards and Ethics Committee. She is on the Coordinating Council of the St. Louis Wellness Council. She is a member of American Psychological Association, Missouri Psychological Association, St. Louis Psychologist, National Wellness Association, Association for Psychological Types, Hypnotherapist Association, the St. Louis Association for Training and Development, and Phi Delta Kappan. She is currently president of Missouri Peer Helpers Association.

Dr. Tindall has written numerous articles concerning communication skills, effective guidance practices, substance abuse, stress management, wellness, teambuilding, leadership training, and eating disorders. She has edited journals on Peer Counseling. She has authored *Peer Power Applying Peer Helping Skills, Book 2: Peer Counseling: An In-depth Look at Training Peer Helpers:* and co-authored *Peer Power: Becoming an Effective Peer Helper, Book 1.* Research projects include communication skills training, self-concept development, group work, social problem solving, peer counseling, stress, wellness, and substance abuse. Her doctoral dissertation was "The Effectiveness of a Wellness Program: Coping with Stress in Schools." She has designed assessment instruments and evaluation materials for the Wellness Program.

She has consulted and done workshops with schools, church groups, hospitals, and businesses such as, McDonnell Douglas, Ralston Purina, Maritz, State of Georgia, Delivery Network, Monsanto, M.C.I., Western Union, St. Louis County Sheriff Department, Trans World Airlines, Metropolitan Sewer District, and A.S.T.D. Topics included a wide range from Wellness, Stress Management, Leadership Training, Classroom Management, Time Management, Drugs and Alcohol, Hypnotherapy, Mid-Life Crisis, Peer Counseling, Communication Skills Training, Career Education, Team Building, Eating Disorder, Care for the Care Giver, and Sexism.

She has received her Ph.D. in psychology from St. Louis University, a Specialist in Counseling in Psychology from Southern Illinois University, Edwardsville, a Master's Degree from the University of Missouri at Columbia, and a B.S. Degree from Southwest Missouri State University in Speech and Political Science. Dr. Tindall is married and lives with her husband and sons in St. Louis County. She enjoys playing golf and writing for leisure activities.

SHIRLEY J. SALMON-WHITE, Ph.D.. Dr. Salmon-White is working in the field of education and counseling as Assistant Supervisor of Student Support Services for the Ferguson-Florissant School District and as a licensed psychologist. She was formerly associated with the Rohen and Associates Psychological Center and currently has her own practice with Creve Coeur Counseling and Psychological Clinic in St. Louis County. She has taught at Washington University, University of Missouri at St. Louis, Webster University, and St. Louis Community College. She has been a consultant for the Missouri Department of Secondary and Elementary Education developing the Missouri Comprehensive Guidance Model and the accompanying activities. She also has been involved in annual training of administrators for the Missouri Principals' Academy. She has been invited to participate in National Educational Leadership Program.

Dr. Salmon-White has been president of the St. Louis Pupil Personnel Administrators, a member of the American Psychological Association, St. Louis Association for Counseling Development, Missouri Association for Counseling and Development, American Association for Learning Disabilities, and the National Association for Pupil Personnel Administrators.

In the early 70s, Dr. Salmon-White started several peer helping programs in the Ferguson-Florissant School District, including a child development center run and staffed by professionals and students, a K-12 program in Deliberate Psychological Education where students systematically helped one another, and a comprehensive program in peer counseling. The Ferguson-Florissant School District has remained a leader in the field of peer helping.

Dr. Salmon-White received her Bachelor and Master's Degrees from the University of Missouri at Kansas City, and her Ph.D. from Indiana State University. She is currently working on her superintendent's license at Southern Illinois University Edwardsville. She is currently living in St. Louis County with her three children, Amie, Scott, and Shannon.

9781559590105